AF519827

Apsarases in Indian Literature

Apsarases in Indian Literature

and

The Legend of Urvaśī and Purūravas

by

Krishnakanta Handique

Decent Books

New Delhi

Published and Printed by:
Decent Books
D-36/A-1, Mohan Garden
Najafgarh Road
New Delhi - 110 059

Distributed by:
D.K. Printworld (P) Ltd.
Regd. office : *'Sri Kunj'*, F-52, Bali Nagar
New Delhi - 110 015
Phones : (011) 545-3975, 546-6019; *Fax* : (011) 546-5926
E-mail: dkprint@4mis.com

ISBN 81-86921-16-8

First Published in India in 2001
© Author

No reproduction or translation of this book or part thereof in any form, except brief quotations, should be made without the written permission of the copyright holder, mentioned above, and the Publishers.

Preface

THIS book on presents a study of the popular traditional legend of Purūravas and Uravaśī in some detailed form. It pays adequate attention to the origin, development and characteristics of the *apsaras* or 'nymphs' in Indo-European and Indian works. Lastly, it tries to deal with the social problem of the *devadāsī*s of a later age.

I was greatly helped and inspired by my friend, philosopher and *guru* Dr. Thaneswar Sarmah, the seniormost Reader in the Sanskrit Department, Gauhati University in the course of my research. I am greatly indebted to him and I shall ever remain grateful to him.

Besides, my *śikṣā-guru*s Dr. M.M Sharma, Dr. A.K. Goswami, Dr. A.C. Barthakuria and Dr. R.N. Sharma also encouraged me to undertake this work and strive diligently towards its completion. I am thankful to all of them. I thank my erstwhile teacher Sjt. Ramchandra Bhattacharya, my associates in the department and my colleagues Dr. Akan Chandra Saikia, Dr. Pradip Gogoi, Prof. Jatin Bora, Prof. Guna Baruah, and Prof. Namal Gogi of Tinsukia College, my student and colleague Mrs. Anupama Mahanta, Prof. Chitralata Phukan, Head of Assamese Department of our college for their encouragement. I would like to mention here the librarians of the K.K. Handique Library, G.U., and J.B. College Library and also Dimbeswar Sarma, a teacher of Narmal School, Jorhat, who helped me procure books for study. I am much indebted to my family members for their constant support.

Krishnakanta Handique

Contents

Abbreviations

ABORI	:	Annals of the Bhandarkar Oriental Research Institute
AG	:	*Agni Purāṇa*
AVS	:	*Atharvaveda Śaunaka Saṁhitā*
BD	:	*Bṛhaddevatā* of Śaunaka
BdP	:	*Brahmāṇḍa Purāṇa*
BhāgP	:	*Bhāgavata Purāṇa*
BrP	:	*Brahma Purāṇa*
BUJ	:	*Journal of Bombay University*
BV	:	*Bhāratiya Vidyā Bhatta* Bombay 7
Ch	:	Chapter
Comm.	:	Commentary
Comm.Vol.	:	Commemoration Volume
ed.	:	Edited by
edn.	:	Edition
ff.	:	following
Fel. Vol.	:	Felicitation Volume
fn.	:	Footnote
HASL	:	*History of Ancient Sanskrit Literature* of MaxMuller (1926)
HCIP	:	*History and Culture of Indian People,*

Published by Bharatiya Vidya Bhavan, Bombay.

HIL	:	*History of Indian Literature* by M. Winternitz
HR	:	*Hymns of the Ṛgveda* by Griffith (1973)
HSL(M)	:	*History of Sanskrit Literature* by Macdonell
HSL(V)	:	*History of Sanskrit Literature* by C.V. Vaidya
HP	:	*Harivaṁśa Purāṇa*
KA	:	*Kauṭilya Arthaśāstra*
KSS	:	*Kathā-sarit-sāgara* of Somadeva
Mbh	:	*Mahābhārata*
MS	:	*Manu-smṛti* (*Manu Saṁhitā*)
MtP	:	*Matsya Purāṇa*
Nir	:	*Nirukta* of Yāska
NM	:	*Nītimañjarī*
p.	:	Page
pp.	:	Pages (Plural)
PPOR	:	*Poet-Philosophers of the Ṛgveda* by C.K. Raja
Raghu	:	*Raghuvaṁśa* of Kālidāsa
Rām	:	*Rāmāyaṇa* of Vālmīki
ṚVVIS	:	*Ṛgveda*, Published by Visveshwarananda Indological Series, Hoshiarpur
ṚV	:	*Ṛgveda Samhitā*
Sarva	:	*Sarvāṇukramaṇī of the Ṛgveda Saṁhitā*
ŚB	:	*Śatapatha Brāhmaṇa*

SK	:	*Skanda Purāṇa*
SR	:	*(The) Seers of the Ṛgveda* by Rahurkar
SV	:	*Sāmaveda Saṁhitā*
V	:	Verse
VāP	:	*Vāyu Purāṇa*
VāmP	:	*Vāmana Purāṇa*
VD	:	*Vedārtha Dīpikā* of Sadguru Śiṣya
ViṣP	:	*Viṣṇu Purāṇa*
VMH	:	*Vedische Mythologie* by Von Hillebrandt
VMM	:	*Vedic Mythology* by Macdonell
VMT	:	*Vedic Mythological Tracts* by Dandekar
VR(M)	:	*Vedic Reader* by Macdonell
VV	:	Verses
VVI	:	*Vaidika Vāñmaya Kā Itihāsa* by Bhagavaddatta
YV	:	*Yajurveda Saṁhitā*

1

Introduction

MYTHS and legends, stories and anecdotes allure the minds of not only the masses but also intellectuals and scholarly persons. Through the ages human imagination has given rise to a vast literature replete with myths and legends, wherein the free thought of men finds easy expression. Sometimes, absurdities surpass the dictates of rationality, only to evoke or rouse interest in the human mind. But that does not prevent the listener or reader from enjoying the myths or legends. Therefore, myths and legends are accepted on all hands irrespective of barriers of caste, creed, race and ethnic group. Thus, every language culture preserves this sort of literature from over ages. And the Indians are no exception to it; rather they have preserved a vast literature abounding with myths, legends, stories, parables, tales and narratives. In fact, no other literature can claim equal footing with Indian literature where this literary form is concerned.

Myths and legends are abundantly found in the folk literature of any and every nation. It forms a component part of the folk culture. The older generation conveys this form of art and literature to the younger generation. The younger folks lend their attentive ear to learn the many myths and legends from their elders. Thus, this piece of literature is carried forward from generation to generation.

The themes of myths and legends are varied. On many occasions, the historical pieces intrude into it. Sometimes, the allegorical stories relating to animals, birds and such other lower beings have hidden moral teachings. Fantasies too, connected with absurd activities of the celestial or semi-celestial beings, find a place in such myths and legends. The *apsarases*, *gandharvas*, *vidyādharas* and *kinnaras* occupy an important place in such myths and legends in Indian literature. In all stages of Indian literature beginning from the *Ṛgveda* down to modern literature, fantastic myths and legends about gods and demi-gods are abundantly found. Some legends become so appealing to the people that the same legend reappears at various stages of the literature, repeatedly changing its outer form and assuming new attire. The legend of Purūravas and Urvaśī appears to be such a piece for it has continued to be a favourite theme throughout our literature. It is, of course, very interesting to follow the course of such a legend and study the same, making a note of all elements, original and peripheral, new innovations and so on relating to such a legend. With that end in view, the legend of Purūravas and Urvaśī is now undertaken for a detailed study.

Sources of our study

Two principal sources are to be mentioned:

(1) Primary or original source which embrace the original Sanskrit texts, commentaries and glosses and modern literary pieces, *kāvyas* and plays, and (2) Secondary or tertiary sources, which include critical writings on the original works noted above. The former can be further sub-divided into four categories : (i) Vedic, (ii) Post-Vedic or Epic-Purāṇic, (iii) Classical works, and (iv) Modern literary (creative) works.

(I) VEDIC

(a) All the Vedic *Saṁhitās*, collection of *mantras*.

(b) All the *Brāhmaṇas* (*Āraṇyakas* and Upaniṣads).

(c) Sūtra literature

(d) Ancillary texts, *Bṛhaddevatā*, and others.

(II) THE TWO EPICS

(a) The *Rāmāyaṇa*

(b) The *Mahābhārata*.

The early major Purāṇas:

(a) *Vāyu*

(b) *Brahmāṇḍa*

(c) *Matsya*

(d) *Mārkaṇḍeya*

(e) *Viṣṇu*

The later major Purāṇas:

(f) *Bhāgavata*

(g) *Brahmā*

(h) *Harivaṁśa*

(i) *Agni*

(j) *Vāmana*

(k) *Brahmavaivartta*

Other minor Purāṇas include *Kālika Purāṇa*.

(III) CLASSICAL SANSKRIT WORKS

(a) *Kāvya* of Aśvaghoṣa, Kālidāsa, Bhaṭṭi, Bhāravī, Māgha and Śrīharṣa (these possess least data and, thus, are not taken for study).

(b) Plays of Kālidāsa — *Vikramorvaśīyam* and *Abhijñāna-Sākuntalam*.

(c) *Kathā-sarit-sagāra* of Somadeva.

(IV) MODERN WORKS: (SELECTED WORKS IN ASSAMESE, BENGĀLĪ AND HINDĪ ONLY)

(a) Poems (see Bibliography)

(b) Plays

(c) *Kāvyas*

(d) Adaptations

Among the Vedic *Saṁhitās*, the *ṚV* stands foremost. It supplies the earliest elements of any Indian myth and legend. Particularly the *ṚV* contains the earliest reference to *apsarases*, including Urvaśī, and the dialogue of Purūravas and Urvaśī, the basis of the legend under study. The *SV* which derives all but 75 hymns from the *ṚV* scarcely bears any information about *apsarases*, while the *YV* and the *AV* do contain some information about the nymphs including Urvaśī. The *Kaṭhaka* and *Maitrāyaṇī* are notable among these. Among the *Brāhmaṇas* it is the *ŚB* which gives the background story of the dialogue hymn (10.95) of the *ṚV*.

Among the other Vedic literature, *BD* and *NM* stand foremost. The *BD* of Śaunaka has described the legend of Purūravas and Urvaśī in full length with the background as found in, for instance, the *ŚB* and *Rām*. Similarly, the *NM* also throws some light on the legend.

The commentaries of Skandasvāmin, Venkaṭamādhava and Sāyaṇa do also try to supply the background for such a legend in their own way.

The second type of original Sanskrit works of the primary category includes the Epics and the Purāṇas. These two types of literature are very vast and, thus, appear to be the mainstay of information on the Indian myths and legends including those of the *apsaras* and the *gandharvas* – the legend Urvaśī among them.

The *Rām* contains valuable legends of Urvaśī and Purūravas in separate pieces. It supplies the background of the birth legend of Vasiṣṭha hinted in the R̥gvedic verses (7, 18, 13-15). It gives the background of Urvaśī's fall from heaven. The birth legend of *apsaras* is also related by it.

The *Mbh* states numerous legends of *apsaras* including that of Urvaśī, which is dealt with briefly. The *apsaras* are said to have originated from Prādhā, a daughter of Dakṣa, a celebrated Prajāpati, married to Kāśyapa, the son of Marīci.

The Purāṇas are known to be a mine of information on the *apsaras* in general and on the legend of Purūravas and Urvaśī in particular. Among the major Purāṇas of the early period, the *Matsya*, the *Vāyu*, the *Viṣṇu* and the *Bhāgavata* have paid adequate attention to describing the legend of Purūravas and Urvaśī. The *Viṣṇu* and the *Bhāgavata* a running commentary upon the *R̥V* dialogue, adding some innovation to the original story. It is the *Vāmana Purāṇa* which describes the birth legend of Urvaśī from the thigh of Nārāyaṇa. The *Devī-Bhāgavata* give also describes the legend perfectly well. Other Purāṇas, the *Brahma*, *Padma*, *Skanda*, *Agni* and *Kūrma*, are found to have vied with one another to focus attention on the popular legend of Purūravas and Urvaśī. These Purāṇas describe numerous legends regarding other *apsaras* too. But most of them originated in post-Vedic literature only.

The *kāvyas* present meagre information about the *apsaras*. But some of the plays have adequately dwelt upon the stories of *apsaras*. The story of Menakā and Viśvāmitra is alluded to in the *Abhijñāna-Śakuntalam*. So, Miśrakeśī or Sānumati has played a minor role in the play. It is the *Vikramorvaśīyam* of Kālidāsa that is based on the famous legend which is our concern. The theme has been handled by the playwright in a magnificent manner, drawing it on a broad canvas with multiple colours. In other words, the legend has been immortalised by Kavikulaguru for ever. From a reading of the drama it appears that Kālidāsa knew the dialogue of the *R̥gveda*, the narration of the *ŚB* and the legends described in the two Epics and in the early Purāṇas. However, some of the works of the later age were influenced by Kālidāsa.

Due to paucity of our knowledge in and about the Prākṛtas we have abstained from that literature and directed our attention to some of the modern works.

Some poets of modern age have composed fine poems taking Urvaśī as the subject. The Nobel laureate Rabindranath Tagore stands foremost among them. Some of the Assamese poets have also composed poems on Urvaśī.

In Hindī literature, Dinkar (Rāmdhārī Singh) is credited with a modern *kāvya* entitled Urvaśī. Although he has deviated from the original in his approach, yet his main theme remains almost the same. We have devoted a section to this work.

So also, Dipak Chandra has composed a prose work known as the *Urvaśī Jananī*. The work is a novel attempt in depicting the theme anew. It has been studied in detail here.

The *Abhiśapta Urvaśī* is a modern play composed by Narayana Kataki in Assamese. Although the work has not been considered as an outstanding piece, the legend of Urvaśī and king Daṇḍin is the mainstay of the play. Thus, it shows deviation from the main current. We have devoted another section to it.

Method and approach

We have hinted above that the wide-ranging literature/literary works are the sources of the legend of Purūravas and Urvaśī. Thus, for the full-scale study of the legend, we have collected materials from various original sources — from the *Ṛgveda* to modern works like the *Abhiśapta Urvaśī*. The materials, thus, collected were analysed and correlated with consistent data and then the conclusion was drawn. We have tried to evaluate the data found in each work, and pointed out wherever and whenever any piece has deviated from the original Vedic story – which is recorded in the Ṛgvedic dialogue with the background set in the *ŚB*. We have tried to find rationality everywhere, discarding or removing any sort of absurdities. A critical assessment of the data is presented in sequel and conclusion/results thereof also are given.

In the process of our study we have found that the original story of Purūravas and Urvaśī has not found total expression in the dialogue of the *Ṛgveda* (X.95). It begins all of a sudden and ends abruptly. It is the *ŚB* that helps us to reconstruct the legend in a consistent way. In this process of reconstruction, Śaunaka's *Bṛhaddevatā* extends valuable help as also do the commentators. The Epics and the Purāṇas appear to have expanded on the theme enshrined in the sacred Vedic texts. The *Viṣṇu* and the *Bhāgavata* began the very process of amplification, as they should do, following the dictum suggested in the verse, *itihāsa-purāṇābhyām vedam samupavṛhayet*. Other Purāṇas too followed suit and gave their versions of the story, remaining mostly faithful to the Vedic version. This trend is found to have been maintained throughout the successive ages. Even Somadeva in his *Kathā-sarit-sāgara*, and Kālidāsa are found to be faithful to the original. The master dramatist, however, made that many changes in the theme as was needed for the legend's adaptation to a drama. In this way, we have followed the course of the story with right earnestness.

Our endeavour is not confined to the story element alone; rather we shall see how it gave rise to the tradition of *devadāsīs* or temple courtesans that has become so much prevalent in the temples of this country. It is assumed that the origin and development of the institution of the *apsaras*es, as discussed in the following pages, will make it clear as to how this institution gave rise to the institution of the temple-courtesans, both sharing many features. Thus, both the institutions were causing social problems, and, hence, approach to them should be made from that angle.

Summary of the present work

The work comprises seven full chapters including the Introduction and the Conclusion, besides a comprehensive Bibliography, hints to abbreviations and an Index of the names of the *apsaras*. Chapters 2-5 form the core of the research.

The first chapter is devoted to a brief inquiry into the origin of the institution of the *apsaras* at the Indo-European stage. Here we have noted briefly the activities of the nymphs in Greek mythology.

The second chapter is more extensive as it deals with the *apsaras* in general, described in the vast ancient literature in Sanskrit beginning from the Vedic *Saṁhitās* to the classical literature. Here again, detailed information from the two Epics, *Rām* and *Mbh* and the major Purāṇas serve as sources. Numerous *apsaras* are met in the long range of Epico-Purāṇic literature and their role in the lives of the gods and men alike appears to be very interesting. The birth or origin of this institution has been traced to the Epico-Purāṇic source.

The third and fourth chapters appear to be the pivotal point around which the work revolves. However, the Vedic literature provides us with little information when compared to the huge Epico-Purāṇic literature in regard to the interesting role of Urvaśī. It is noted that the R̥gvedic hymn (X.95) and the *ŚB* (V.1, 1) serve as the rock-bed of the Urvaśī saga and the Epics and the Purāṇas have drawn much inspiration from these, the oldest sources, and they have done marvellous work in making the legend/legends about the nymph and her paramour, Purūravas more appealing to the masses of India in particular, and of the world in general. The various versions of the one and the same legend tell us how much of popularity it has enjoyed for a long time in this country.

But it was, however, the great Indian poet Kālidāsa who immortalised this Vedic legend in one of his master-pieces, viz., the *Vikramorvaśīyam*. It goes without saying that this play had a great role in popularising the legend among Indians, for dramatisation serves as the means of mass-communication through which such things earn popularity. However, we have noted the innovation the poet has brought in when dramatising the original story without affecting its mainstream.

Again we have here dealt with some of the interesting works done in modern Indian literature. Among these Dinkar's epic *Urvaśī* is epoch-making.

There is no dearth of stray poetic works on the subject in modern literature, although we have restricted ourselves here to the independent and original works.

In the sixth chapter we have examined and discussed the problem of the *devadāsī*s, a tradition which we suspect originated from the institution of *apsara*s as noted above.

Part I
Apsarases in Indian Literature

2

Origin and Development of Apsarases

Origin of the nymphs in Indo-European literature

THE philologists among other oriental scholars[1] hold the view that the Indians and Europeans have a common origin for their language, literature and, above all, for their culture. Those who have dealt with the comparative mythology[2] have pointed out some features shared by the early Indo-Āryans and the Europeans, particularly the Greeks. Studies have shown some resemblance of nymphs in both the mythologies which is very striking.[3] This is true in the case of other mythologies of the nations of Europe, like the Roman, the Tutonic and the Scandinavian as well. The genesis of the *apsaras*es or nymphs also form a common theme for the Indian and European mythologists. Our Indian literature beginning from the *Ṛgveda* down to the present-day prose, poetry and plays are replete with episodes connected with the *apsaras*es. The beauty of Urvaśī, Rambhā and Menakā is praised and presented by our modern writers too. The modern poets and litterateurs of Europe include mention of the nymphs. Heinrich Heine[4] is a glaring example. In one of his works, Heine has described as to how the song of a nymph charmed a boatman who succumbed to an accident eventually.[5]

The nymphs are generally said to have inhabited springs, rivulets, rivers, groves of trees, and mountains, which lie outside the human habitat; they are differentiated from the goddesses, who are said to be the wives of gods. Because the nymphs are found to be attached to a particular spot, each spring has its own nymphs. Some nymphs belong to the ocean, and they are called the daughters of the ocean. They are said to be found in the Mediterranean parts of the world. As the nymphs belong to waterbodies like the rivers, lakes and springs, they are designated by the general name 'Naidaes' (in Greek, *naō* means 'flow'). Some nymphs are said to have powers and inspired men with the same, and to confer upon them the gift of poetry. But popular belief continued among the Greeks and Romans that a mortal who chanced to see a nymph was bereft of sense.

According to the belief prevalent among the Indo-European people, the nymphs could be classified according to the places they belonged to. Thus, there were nymphs of mountains, nymphs of forests, and nymphs of trees, and those in special habitats who abide in watery glades, caves and old groves.[6] They have been worshipped with goats, lambs, milk and oil. With regard to the nymphs, the name of Circe and Calypso,[7] who were divine in nature but differed from goddesses, comes to mind but they have presided over the isles of Circe. They were represented as fully clothed but gradually they came to be shown less clothed and finally wholly naked. They are said to be related to Pan and Hermes, and other significant characters of Greek literature. Although Aphrodite[8] appears to be a goddess in Greek literature, she also resembles the nymphs for she is said to have sprung from the foam of the sea according to Greek mythology. Thetis[9] was a pure water nymph who had released Zeus and had brought the hundred Briasseus of Acquaca to help him.

Among the gods, Pan is associated with the nymphs, and with them he shares dedication.[10] He is a god of shepherd and huntsmen, who is described to have invented the flute with seven reeds which he called syrinx. Although the nymphs possessed divine powers and had longevity, they could not enjoy immortality and had no temple as their abode. Such nymphs are said to have caused madness, a kind of which is called Nymphlepsy. Nymphlepsy may also be a form of prophetic inspiration.[11]

Eurydice[12] is a wood nymph with whom Orpheus, a legendary pre-Homeric poet and a flute-player, made love. Unfortunately he lost her due to the bite of a snake and tried utmost to restore her but failed to keep his promise made before. Pluto and Persephone and lost her. Out of ardent love for Eurydice and being of a sensitive nature he offended the women of Thrace and was torn to pieces but his head which still uttered the name of Eurydice was thrown into the river Hebrus.

In a word it may be said that love of nature among the Greeks and Romans prevailed from the primitive ages and many songs were composed in the form of hymns. Instances are not rare to cite especially with reference to Aphrodite, who was the goddess of fertility in the minds of the Greeks and the Romans.[13] The opinion of a scholar like M. Winternitz[14] may be given with regard to this.

Summing up the discussion, we may state that the nymphs found in the Indo-European literature have affinity with the *apsaras*es belonging to Indian literature though they present a contrast in some cases.

Characteristics of nymphs

A number of scholars belonging to the East and West[15] have expressed various opinions with regard to the characteristics of *apsaras*es or nymphs.[16] A class of celestial damsels who resided in the sky were regarded as the wives of the *gandharva*s. They are said to be very fond of bathing, capable of changing their form and endowed with superhuman power. They are called *svarveśyāḥ* and are generally described as the servants of Indra. The word is usually found in plural.

Sir Monier-Williams takes *āpaḥ* (*Āpah*) in the sense of 'water', 'air' as the intermediate region, and *naif* meaning 'water nymphs', the starlight virgins.[17]

And according to Manu the *apsaras* symbolised the clouds or the mists drawn up by the Sun. The *apsaras*es have power to assume any form at their will. Many instances of this are found in the post-Vedic literature.[18] They can change their form like *rākṣasas* and often appear as aquatic birds. It is believed that when warriors die in the battlefield they are taken by the *apsarases* in brilliantly-coloured chariots.

Scholars opine that they are semi-divine beings and consorts of gods.

The *apsarases* are inferior divinities of nature. They especially dwell in groves of forests and caves, besides streams and rivers and in some cases in lonely places such as islands, like Calypso and Circe in Greek myths. In this context we may point out that Greek literature also presents them as a kind of spirits who inhabit the hills, forests and meadows, and thereby are called in Homer's works, daughters of Zeus, while on the other hand, Hesiod makes the nymphs of the hills and the forests benevolent spirits, who lead a life of liberty — sometimes weaving in groves, sometimes dancing and singing with Artemis and others or revealing with Dionysus.[19]

Apsarases relation with the gandharvas

Scholars opine that the *apsarases* have a close relation with the *gandharvas*. Special names of the *gandharvas* like Citraratha, Vasuratha and Suratha, often occur in texts. There is a vivid description of the role of the *gandharvas* in the *Ṛgveda* who accompanied by the *apsarases* are said to have brought *soma* (rain). In the post-Vedic literature their names are often found to be associated with various myths. Citraratha is almost invariably described as the king of the *gandharvas* in the *Mbh* and the *Rām*, and in the Purāṇas. The *gandharvas*, in later mythological works, are devoid of their elementary nature, in contrast to what is found in Vedic literature, and at last they are said to be musicians in the Paradise of Indra, and they constitute a different class of semi-divine beings. The *apsarases* do not appear to have any anthropomorphic traits of their own inasmuch as they have been usually shown as exceedingly beautiful damsels from the early period. They have been depicted as the instrument of joy and merriment among the gods after the defeat of the Maras. The apsarases are four in number in the Bharhut relief. They are as follows:

(a) Miśrakeśī

(b) Alaṁbusā

(c) Subhadrā

(d) Padmāvatī

They appear in the style of beautiful damsels and, in a very similar way, are represented in Indian art in later times.

With regard to the characteristics of the *apsaras*es Indian scholars have gone further to discover affinity with the depictions of contemporary writers and scholars of the world. They are female dancers,[20] experts in casting side glances and singing songs at the same time. Moreover, they are described as being uncommonly beautiful with lotus eyes, slender waists and swelling hips, striking ravishing poses and sweet in conversation. They rob the spectators' thought and intellect. It is said that the lotus-eyed *apsaras*es with huge hips and buttocks and attractive breasts steal the thoughts and senses of the beholder with their beauty and grace.

Scholars like Fausbal[21] have given an elaborate list of the *apsaras*es, who are mentioned in the works of post-Vedic times. They are Miśrakeśī, Rambhā, Citrasenā, Cusmittā, Cārunetrā, Gr̥htācī, Menakā, Pramlocā, Urvaśī, Irā, Vargā, Sañjā, Vudvudā, Hirā, Parvacitti, Svayamprabhā, Daṇḍagurī, Varuthinī, Sahajanyā-Kambhayanī, Citralekhā, Svāhā, Madhusvarā, Citrāṅgadā, Ruci, Monaharā, Sukésī, Sumukhī, Hastinī, Prabhā, Dāntā, Vidyutā and Rati and others.

The *apsaras*es are described as supernatural beings[22] and although they stand as enemies, yet in most cases they appear friendly to mankind. They are able to see something in the mortal world by virtue of the magical or supernatural powers which they possess. They try to allure others with their music and song. In doing so, they come out successful but sometimes they become prey to the curses of the seers. Many instances of this are found in the post-Vedic works.

The word *apsaras*es[23] appears to be related to the word *apsaras*, conveying its opposite. Picchel has interpreted the word 'Psraras' as foam, and *apsaras* would naturally mean 'foamers'. P. Banerjee[27] testifies that *apsaras* signify clouds, and wherever the *Ṛgveda* mentions the word *apsaras* it indicates the cloud. P. Banerjee[28] has collected various kinds of information and opinions in his famous work which has revealed his unique aptitude inhabited the heaven of Sakka. According to the Buddhist work they are called *acchara*, the Pāli equivalent of the Vedic *apsaras*es. They are Nandā, Sunandā, Sakattimā, Alambuṣā, Miśrakeśī, Handvvilla, and others. They are friends of Sakka, because they shut the doors of salvation by deceptive delight. Sometimes Sakka sends them to earth to the ascetics, who by virtue of their penance ascend in the heaven. Once he sent the nymphs for alluring the Buddhisattaka in a musical contest by dancing to the tune of his lyre.

The beautiful *apsaras*es not only occupy a major place in Indian literature, but they are also depicted with all sorts of erotic suggestions. Their erotic postures and movements are able to evoke erotic *rasa* or flavour or sentiment in the minds of readers and spectators. Along with their description, they are shown with a bare bosom and waist and also their nude abdomen are not covered by any apparel. The sculptures depict them in various poses with uncovered physic. Sometimes they are shown with a deep navel and the two things below it are closely attached, and the lower garment has been worn practically from the upper part of the thighs so that their genitals are half-exposed. They are shown as gently supporting one breast with their palm and lost in beholding its seductive charms with indulgence. And sometimes they are loosening their lower garments, thereby exposing themselves. Often there is a very subtle erotic suggestion in these simple sculptures: they are shown with a number of nail marks on the breasts and near the armpit as found in the Lakṣmaṇa temple.[24]

In this context we may cite Bhāravi, who has delineated the role of the *apsaras*es in detail. He has shown their erotic gesticulations in order to entice Arjuna in the penance grove, so that the latter might be dissuaded from the path of stern penance undertaken to win the Pāśupata missile from Lord Śiva. It may be added that in temple architecture, the erotic scenes were carved vividly where human models were not available at all. The norms of beauty and expression of erotic and seductive attitudes were models. It is found that although the temples of central India did not suggest gross sex, they never forgot to suggest the sport and delight of the premorbid energy.

Scholars like M. Winternitz also suggest that these *apsaras*es and *gandharva*s of the ancient Indian tradition correspond in every respect, in an amazing manner, with the spirits, elves and fairies of popular belief.

So also S.A. Dange remarks that the *apsaras*es have a role in the ritual of Agnicayana with reference to *mithuna*. The *apsaras*es are closely associated with water and fertility and were originally of more significance in early literature than in later literature. They were called minor divinities. The famous poet Bhāsa has remarked that the *apsaras*es dwell in the upper region of the Himālayas — the region known as Uttarakuru is the abode of the beautiful *apsaras*es. The famous sculptors opine that when sculpting the artistic imagination and thoughts were latent in their minds, and thereby they carved on a separate strip or panel or marble. They were used to decorate the fountain of innocents in Parish. It is said that the *apsaras*es wield great influence over rural folks who generally inhabit the hilly and the forest regions, for the dance art of nymphs, which has been traditionally handed over to them, has greatly impressed their imaginative and artistic mind. It is obvious that they also influenced the dancers, poets, painters and sculptors for ages.

Amarsiṁha, author of *Amarakoṣa*,[25] has remarked that along with Urvaśī, the other nymphs are celestial dancers and courtesans of *svarga*.

From an assessment of the various opinions referred to above with regard to the characteristics of the *apsarases*, it may be said with affirmation that women or *prakṛti* (Nature) is man's elixir of life. An *apsarā* who is one of the elements of nature and part of woman kind sings allowing gesticulations, i.e., is a '*nartakī*' dancer who may be called a cosmic dancer — who dances before the *puruṣa* in a voluntary display of her dynamic capacities[26]. In brief it may be summarised that all the essential qualities of womanhood are present in the *apsarā*, because she is the elixir of life, full of sentiments, grace, beauty and charm. She is goddess of fertility and progeny, and above all she conducts all-worldly processes and activities. She is, as a matter of fact, the chief force of energy. So there cannot be any hesitation in asserting that *apsarā* is essentially a woman.[27]

Origin of the nymphs or apsarases in Indian literature

Several scholars[28] of India and outside have put forward different views with reference to the nymphs or *apsarases* who occupy a less important place in the *ṚV* in comparison to the *AV*. The *apsarases* denote a kind as nymph that even in the *ṚV* appears almost completely separated from her physical basis. The information there obtainable is very scanty as the name occurs only five times.

The Ṛgvedic hymn (VII.33) has described the legend of the birth of Vasiṣṭha and Agastya[29] in the same breath. In the *ṚV* (VII.33.9) the *apsarases* are said to have brought Vasiṣṭha hither wearing the vesture spun for them by Yama. In the verse 110 the double birth of Vasiṣṭha[30] is indicated: when Mitra and Varuṇa saw him as light coming out that was one birth and in the other, Vasiṣṭha was led by Agastya to the Pratardas.

The verse 11-B pointedly refers to the birth of Vasiṣṭha and the name of Uravśī is mentioned as the mother (in verse II).[31]

In *ṚV*, X.123.5 the poet says that the *apsarā* smiles at her beloved (*gandharva*) and supports him in the sublimest heaven.[32] Griffith tries to identify the *apsaras* with celestial nymphs who symbolise the waters of heaven. In *R̥V* IX.78.3, it is said that the *apsaras*es who dwell in sea waters have flowed Soma wise of heart. They urge the master of the house upon his way and, to the eternal Pavamāna, pray for bliss.[33]

In *R̥V* X.136.6 again we find mention of the *apsaras*es with the *gandharva*s. They are here described as the sylvan beasts.[34]Thus, according to the R̥gvedic seers, *apsaras*es and *gandharva*s are connected with waters and sylvan groves.

APSARASES IN THE ATHARVAVEDA

In comparison to the *R̥gveda* the *AV* has frequent references to the *aparases*.[39] they are mentioned as coming and going (from their abode in the waters) in a thrice.[40]

The *apsaras*es are generally associated with the *gandharvas*[41]and known for their intimacy with them. They are referred to as the wives of the *gandharva*s. Viśvāvasu,[42] the *gandharva* king, is their leader. They are connected with clouds, lightning and stars. Again, the *apsaras*es may be said to be the lovers of the *gandharva*s.[43]

The *apsaras*es are said to have dwelt in the waters.[44] They assumed the character of being the womenfolk of the *gandharva*s in later *Saṁhitā*s.

Some scholars say that in course of time the *apsaras*es had to extend their abode on the earth and they started inhabiting the trees in particular.

They are said to inhabit banyan or *nyagrodha* and sacred fig trees *aśvattha* in which their cymbals and lutes resound. They are especially spirits of nature, rivers and forests. Rivers are one of their usual dwelling places.

It is said that when a wedding procession has to pass by such trees, they have to be propitiated in the trees, so that there may not arise any misfortune or disaster to the newly married couple.[45]

The *AV* adds some traits to the *apsaras*es. They are said to be fond of dice and bestow luck on players but they are feared as they may cause derangement and, therefore, magic is employed against them.[46]

The *apsaras*es are invoked to bring lovers who have remained at a distance closer, and they are said to be the protectors of cattle and prosperity.

There are a few *sūktas*[47] in the *AV* which offer cures for illnesses, such as insanity and poisoning which are supposed to be caused by the *gandharva*s and the *apsaras*es. They are supposed to have some spirits and in order to drive away their spirits, the ancient Indian magicians made use of a pleasant smelling plant called *agaśṛṅgī* (*odina pinnata*) and recited incantations. The *AV* says that the *apsaras*es and *gandharva*s protect mortal beings.[48]

The *ṛṣi*s invoke the *gandharva*s and the *apsaras*es along with Agni.[49]

The *AV* says[50] that the *gandharva*s and the *apsaras*es, *rākṣasa*s, *piśāca*s are the enemies of the mortal world. While praising *vanaspati*s, the *gandharva*s and the *apsaras*es, who are suppose to have manifested themselves in the *vanaspati*s, are eulogised.[51]

During the funeral performance, Agni is invoked so that through his help the mortal being may get the favour of Urvaśī and other *apsaras*es in heaven.[52]

APSARASES IN THE YAJURVEDA

Like the *ṚV* and the *AV* the *SV* also refers to Urvaśī in particular. The legend of Urvaśī is described in the third chapter.[53] In the *YV*[54] some of the *apsaras*es have been addressed as the representatives of some directions (regions) and sub-directions (sub-regions). They are addressed and propitiated in connection with *Agniciti*, enumerated in relation to the seasons, *Vasanta*, *Grīṣma*, *Varṣā*, *Śarat*, *Hemanta* and *Śiśira*. In the front region and direction, i.e., east two *apsaras*es, Puñjikasthalā and Kratusthalā are paid homage among others. To the south two other *apsaras*es, Menakā and Sahajanyā are prayed to. To the west two other *apsarases*, Pramalocā and Anumlocā are paid homage. Similar reverence is paid to Viśvācī and Ghṛtācī in the north direction, while Urvaśī and Pūrvacitti are prayed above and below. They are connected with the six seasons mentioned above in successive order. The commentators Uvaṭa and Mahidhara have tried to offer etymological meaning to each of the names of the *apsarases*.[55] This kind of an approach is rarely seen in other works. From a perusal of the etymological meanings offered by the commentators it appears that (1) the *apsarases* possess beautiful form, (2) they evoke desire (sexual) in the heart of men (males) and (3) they are common to all. Again in the *YV* XVIII.38-43, the *gandharvas* and the *apsarases* are referred to as the adjuncts of Agni, Sūrya and others. In V.38, Agni is identified with the *gandharvas* and the *apsarases* with rays which are called *ayava*, 'protective power'. In verse 40, radiance of the Sun, i.e., *Candramas* is identified with the *gandharvas* while the luminaries (*nakṣatrāṇi*) are identified with the *apsarases*, which are also called 'the object reflecting rays' (*bhekurayaḥ*). In V.21, the wind is identified with the *gandharvas*, while waters with the *apsarases*, which are also called strength (*urjās*). In V.42 Suparṇa sacrifice is identified with the *gandharvas*, while the honorarium (*dakṣiṇā*) is identified with the *apsarases*, which are also called praisers (*stava*). In verse 43 Prajāpati Viśvakarman and wind are identified with the *gandharvas*, while the *Ṛkas* and *Sāmans* are identified with the *apsarases*, which are called desires (*iṣṭayaḥ*). Thus, the *gandharvas* and the *apsarases* are put up as pairs in describing various deities in the *YV* (*Śukla*).[56]

Apsarases in the Rāmāyana : Post-Vedic Period

One version of the origin of the *apsarases* is described in the *Rām* of Vālmikī.[57] It is said that during the churning of the ocean by the gods and the demons (*asuras*), the beautiful damsels rose out of the juices, and, therefore, they are called *apsarases*.[58] They were seven crore in number. Their attendants were also numerous.[59] They were wedded neither by the gods nor by the *asuras*. So, they remained as the common wives (*sādhāraṇa-strī*) or as common property of both the gods and the demons.[60]

VARIOUS LEGENDS OF THE APSARASES IN THE RĀM.

Besides the origin of the *apsaras*es, Vālmikī describes a good number of myths and legends about the *apsaras*es, which are found in various chapters of the seven *kāṇḍa*s in the Rām.[61] Some of the myths are related to the *apsaras*es in connection with the sages of these times who were engrossed in deep penance and meditation.[62]

The famous legend of Menakā and Viśvāmitra is given in the *Rām*[63] as follows:

> Once upon a time, a bitter feud took place between Viśvāmitra and Vasiṣṭha owing to the heavenly cow Kāmadhenu, which was reared by the latter with earnestness and devotion. However, Viśvāmitra was overcome by the armies created by Nandinī (Kāmadhenu). Having being humiliated thus, Viśvamitra did severe penance. Seeing this Indra became frightened and he sent Menakā, one of the beautiful *apsaras*es, to disturb his penance. Viśvāmitra was charmed by her beautiful form, gesticulation and dance. Also, he saw her when she had taken bath in the sacred waters of Puṣkara and was bewitched by her fascinating beauty. He discarded all self-control and took her to his hermitage.[72] He passed ten long years with Menakā. As a result of their union, Menakā gave birth to Śakuntalā, whose story is described in the *Mbh*[64] and later immortalised by Kālidāsa[65] in his drama *Abhijñāna-Śākuntalam*.

RAMBHĀ AND VIŚVĀMITRA

Rambhā's seduction of Viśvāmitra is also described in the *Rām*[66]as follows:

> Viśvāmitra's mind was stung with remorse and shame as he had uselessly spent his time and energy with Menakā. He discarded her and resorted to penance

again and become a great seer, but failed to achieve *Brahmattva*. He left no stone unturned. He again resorted to severe penance to attain *Brahmattva*. Again this time Indra stood against him on his way and sent another nymph, Rambhā by name, to seduce the seer. Indra promised to send Cupid and the spring season to help her in her mission. Rambhā began to sing rapturous songs in accompaniment to the cuckoo's note. The cuckoo was none other than Indra himself. Viśvāmitra was at first delighted at the hearing of the sweet voice, but later he thought it might be an intrigue perpetrated by Indra and so he cursed her (Rambhā) to become a marble stone and remain so for ten thousand years. The happy episode turned into a tragedy for Rambhā.

NATURAL ROLE OF THE APSARASES

The *apsaras*es played a major role in thwarting the goals of many persons – sages, heroes and others. Through their songs, dances and love intrigues, they often descended to the mortal world with a view to take part in marriage festivals, for example, in the marriage ceremony of Rāmacandra and Sītā which was held in Janaka's capital (Mithilā), and in the birth festivals of noble and noted heroes. Many such instances are found in later literature as well.

During the marriage ceremony of Rāma and Sītā, heavenly music was heard emanating/pouring from the above and flowers were showered from the sky. A host of *apsaras*es started their dance with the music played by *gandharvas*.[67]

The *apsaras*es and the *gandharva*s are found taking delight in witnessing the heroic activities of the famous heroes engaged in fighting in the battlefields. Such an instance is the great duel between Paraśurāma and Rāmacandra, which took place in Janaka's palace. On that occasion a host of *apsaras*es, *gandharva*s, *siddha*s, *cāraṇa*s, *kinnara*s, *rākṣasa*s and *nāga*s descended to witness the heroic deeds of the two famous heroes, with lofty speech to praise their bravery in war.[68-69]

APSARASES' ROLE IN THE HERMITAGE OF BHARADVĀJA

The *Rām*[70] describes in detail the role of the *apsaras*es in the *āśrama* of the great sage Bharadvāja.

After banishment, Rāma, Lakṣmaṇa and Sitā stayed in the hermitage of Bṛharadvāja for a night and then left for Citrakūṭa. Bharata, accompanied by Vasiṣṭha and others and followed by a big army, went to meet his elder brother Rāma. They met Guhaka, who helped Bharata and his followers in crossing the Ganges with his boats. Bharadvāja was aware of the manner and customs pertaining to proper reception and entertainment of royal guests. At the arrival of the royal guests with a host of dignitaries and followed by a large army, Bharadvāja resolved to accord a befitting reception. So the sage entered the chamber of his sacrificial fire and, having washed his hands and feet twice with water, invoked god Viśvakarman and other heavenly creatures along with the *apsaras*es to help him in his great endeavour.[71]

After the invocation, heavenly music was heard, the *apsaras*es began to dance and the *gandharva*s to sing. At that time twenty thousand women sent by Prajāpati and another twenty thousand sent by Kubera adorned with pearls and gems appeared on the scene and created a flutter by their beauty. Then came another twenty thousand damsels from the heavenly Nandana forest accompanied by *gandharva* king, Nanda. Then Tamburu and Śāpa began to sing before Bharata. Miśrakeśī and other heavenly damsels began to dance.[72]

EPISODE OF VIRĀDHA

It is said in the *Rām*[73] that a *gandharva* Tamburu by name was cursed, and he had to descend as *rākṣasa* Virādha. During the exile of Rāma, Lakṣmaṇa and Sītā in the forest, Virādha had forcibly carried away Sītā and challenged Rāma and Lakṣmaṇa to a duel. Rāma killed him with utmost power. But at the touch of Rāma the *rākṣasa* could remember his previous birth. He said to Rāma the following words:

> My name is Tamburu and I am a *gandharva*. I once failed to attend upon Kubera, the lord of the *yakṣas*, when I was absent from my duty on account of my attachment to Rambhā. Lord Kubera cursed me to be born as a *rākṣasa*, saying that when king Daśaratha's son Rāma would slay me in the battlefield I should get back my former state of *yakṣa*.

MANDĀKINĪ AND PAÑCĀPSARASES

A story[74] relates the origin of the five *apsaras*es. Once upon a time when Rāma, Lakṣmaṇa and Sītā happened to visit a hermitage (of Dharmavit), they heard the story from the hermit Dharmavit himself. There was a lake in which five *apsaras*es took shelter. In the time of antiquity, Mandākinī, a sage, practised severe penance for ten thousand years seated in the pool. The gods were frightened by the rigorous penance of the sage, and they engaged the five *apsaras*es to dissuade the hermit from his penance. The *ṛṣi* fell prey to his passions and he made those nymphs his wives. Mandākinī became young by virtue of his yogic powers and built a secret chamber to keep these five *apsaras*es. When people passsed by the side of that chamber of the sage and the damsels, they used to hear the sound of dance and music coming from inside the lake. As the five *apsaras*es were living in that pool, they became known as Pañcāpsarases.

PUÑJIKASTHALĀ : MOTHER OF HANUMĀN

It is said in the *Rām*[75] that Puñjikasthalā, mother of Hanumān, the commander-in-chief of Rāma, was originally a nymph. A story of her was retold by Jāmbavat, the bear chief of the ape army, which runs as follows:

Once there was a beautiful nymph named Puñjikasthalā who was also known as Añjanā. She was wife of monkey king Keśarī and daughter of Kuñjara. Spotless Añjanā was famous for her beauty in the three worlds; there was none to equal her beauty on earth. But on account of a curse she was born in the Vānara (ape) family, yet having heavenly virtues innate in her she could assume any form at her will.

Once Añjanā in her youthful beauty was strolling about along the green hills. She had adorned herself with fine ornaments, wore yellow robes with pink borders and had an excellent garland on her neck. The wind god gently wafted the garment of the large-eyed Añjanā, baring her plump thighs, slim waist, heavy hips and stout breasts. God Vāyu was charmed by her beauty and embraced her amorously. Chaste Añjanā was alarmed by this and nervously asked who was, thus, seducing her. Thereupon the wind god told her not to be afraid of him, who never sought to harm her at all. He consoled her that he would enter her body only in thought, and assured her that in due time she would give birth to a strong and intelligent son like him. Thus, Añjanā got pleasure coming in contact with the wind-god and in course of time she gave birth to a son in a cave. Once when the boy saw the Sun rising in the sky, he took him to be an edible thing and soared high in the sky. At that time he sprang up three hunderd *yojanas*, yet he was not discomforted by the heat of the sun. The king of the gods (Indra) saw him, thus, proceeding in great speed along the sky and becoming angry, hurled the thunderbolt upon him. Being struck by the thunderbolt he fell down on a rock and his left jaw was broken and, thus, he was called Hanumān.

There is another similar episode relating to the birth of Hanumān in the said epic.[76] It states that Rāvaṇa became too powerful to easily defeat all the gods, *gandharvas*, *siddhas*, sages and also *apsarases*.[77] And, thus, being humiliated by Rāvaṇa, the *apsarases*, along with the *devarṣis*, *gandharvas* and *rudras*, propitiated Lord Viṣṇu for a remedy. At that time Lord Brahmā advised the gods that they should give birth to some indomitable heroes through union with *apsarases*, the wives of the *yakṣas*, the daughters of the *nāgas* (serpents), and wives of the *ṛṣis* and *vidyādharas*.

REFERENCE TO GHṚTĀCĪ AND VIŚVĀMITRA

It is stated in the *Rām*[78] that after Sugrīva was consecrated as the king of Kiṣkindhā, he forgot all about the treaties he had made with Rāma. He was engrossed totally in worldly pleasure. At this Lakṣmaṇa was enraged and he met Sugrīva. He reminded him of the contract he had made with Rāma for searching out Sītā. Sugrīva was ashamed of his behaviour and being frightened he sent Tārā, his wife, to pacify Lakṣmaṇa with gentle words. Tārā referred to the incident of Ghṛtācī with whom Viśvāmitra eloped forgetting his severe austerity. And she reminded him of the deplorable condition of the self-controlled Viśvāmitra who had to spend ten long years with Ghṛtācī, who is said to be the mother of Kuṣanābha's daughters,[79] and could somehow free himself from her lustful clutches only with a great effort.

PLACES INFESTED BY THE APSARARSES

During the long search for the whereabouts of Sītā Sugrīva had lots of experiences. He had a chance to discover the Kṣīroda ocean which was full of swans and gods, *yakṣas* and the *cāraṇas*. It was also visited by the *vānaras* and nymphs for amorous sports.[80]

MALAYA MOUNTAIN

Sugrīva directed his troops of monkeys to trace the whereabouts of Sītā, with his focus on the Malaya mountain which was full of sandalwood, flowery trees and plants on the transparent Kāverī. The nymphs always sported in its stream. He said that this mountain was also an abode of the heavenly nymphs, *yakṣas* and *cāraṇas*, and even the king of gods, Indra visited that place.[81]

KAILĀSA

It is also reported in the *Rām* that on the Kailāsa mountain there was a lake full of lotuses, it was visited by swans and ducks and nymphs sported in its water. The Uttarakuru was one of the finest places frequented by the virtuous people.[82] According to the description found in the *Rām* of Vālmiki,[83] there were some beautiful gardens here full of palatable food, delicious drinks and beautiful and accomplished damsels who roamed there.

UDAYAGIRI

The Udayagiri was also visited by the nymphs according to the description given by Sugrīva in the *Rām.*[84]

HEMĀ

While Hanumān and his companions were busy in search of Sītā they chanced to discover an ascetic woman in a deep cave. She was none other than Svayamprabhā, a nymph.[85] She told them that she was married to Mayadānava who was known as Viśvakarman among the *dānavas*. This cave belonged to Hemā, an *apsarā* who was a friend of hers, but she had to vacate it on some grounds. Svayamprabhā helped Hanumān come out of the cave by virtue of her magical power. To this episode another romantic episode is added in the Assamese version of the *Mbh* by Rāma Sarasvatī, a renowned poet of the Vaiṣṇava era, who flourished in the post-Śaṅkaradeva period.[86]

HEMĀ : MOTHER OF MANDODARĪ

In the *Rām*, it is reported that once while Rāvaṇa was busy in his victorious journey he had a chance to meet Mayadānava with his beautiful daughter Mandodarī. And in course of conversation Mayadānava said that Mandodarī was his own daughter. She was given birth to by Hemā, as *apsarsā*, as a result of her union with him. Then Mandodarī was given in marriage to Rāvaṇa on that spot.[87]

STORY OF ṚṢYAŚṚṄGA

For a long time king Daśaratha of Ayodhyā was issueless. At the advice of his priests, Daśaratha arranged a *putreṣṭi-yajña* (sacrifice desiring son). To officiate in that sacrifice he chose

Ṛṣyaśṛṅga, the son of Bibhāṇḍaka, as the priest. In that context, the birth story of Ṛṣyaśṛṅga is given. Once Urvaśī, the divine nymph, appeared before Bibhāṇḍaka, who was doing penance in water. He was attracted to her and could not resist his passion for her. His generative fluid fell in the river water where downstream a doe was drinking water out of thirst. The doe drank water with the seminal fluid of the sage and as a result she became pregnant. In due course of time she gave birth to a son. The boy later became renowned as Ṛṣyaśṛṅga, with two horns on his head.[88]

STORY OF ŚABARĪ

The *Rām*[89] describes how Rāma and Lakṣmaṇa met Śabarī when they were wandering in search of Sītā who had been abducted by Rāvaṇa in the dense forest. Śabarī received them with devotion and offered some wild fruits (*badarī*). It is said that Śabarī was none other than an *apsarā* named Citralekhā in her previous birth, and she was the daughter of a *gandharva* named Vitihotra. But as she had illicit love for a hunterman, she had to become a hunterwoman (Śabarī). She received Rāma and Lakṣmaṇa with firm devotion, and by the grace of Rāma was at last released from her sinful bondage.

RAMBHĀ AND RĀVAṆA

Apsarā Rambhā[90] was betrothed to Nala-Kubera, son of Kubera. Once she was forcibly raped by Rāvaṇa who discarded all her prayers and requests, and for his licentious manner, he was cursed by Nala-Kubera that in future, whenever he would try to rape a woman, his heads would be immediately smashed into seven pieces.

RĀVAṆA'S RECOLLECTIONS

During the mortal war with Rāma Rāvaṇa had to arouse Kumbhakarṇa from deep sleep and he felt that his death was impending at the hands of Rāma in the battlefield. He recollected the past events about the nymphs. "Moreover goddess Umā, Nandikeśvara and Varuṇa's daughter, Puñjikasthalā and Rambhā cursed me in such a manner that I do how perceive its consequences," he said in despair.[91]

ROLE OF THE NYMPHS IN THE BATTLEFIELD

The *Rām*[92] describes as to how Meghanāda, the eldest and valiant son of Rāvaṇa, was slain in a fierce battle by Lakṣmaṇa. At his death the gods, *ṛṣis*, *gandharva*s and also the nymphs in the sky repeatedly shouted victory to Lakṣmaṇa. Then the gods in the heaven blew the trumpet of victory and the nymphs are said to have begun to dance in joy. When the fierce battle between Rāma and Rāvaṇa started, the denizens of heaven got frightened by that fearful fight. "May good befall on brāhmaṇas and cows. May Rāvaṇa fall at that dreadful contest," the *gandharva*s and nymphs said.

HERMITAGE OF TṚṆAVINDU

The hermitage of Tṛṇavindu was situated near the Sumeru mountain where, during his stay, daughters of the *ṛṣis*, *nāga*s, and the *apasarase*s used to sport about.[93]

LAṄKĀ : ABODE OF NYMPHS

As stated in the *Rām*, during the reign of Kubera, Laṅkā grew prosperous. Gods and the *gandharva*s sang in honour of his glory and the nymphs danced in his abode. The abode of Kubera as described in the *Rām*[94] resounded with the songs and dances of the nymphs.

PRAYER OF HANUMĀN

It is also reported in the *Rām*[95] that after the destruction of Rāvaṇa, Rāma along with his monkey troops and others returned to Ayodhyā. The victorious one became joyous and he was consecrated on the throne of Ayodhyā, while all his friends along with Sugrīva and others repaired to their respective abode with ample blessings and presents. But Hanumān, the commander-in-chief and trusted devotee of

Rāma, expressed his wish, "Let me live here so long as the story of Rāma will last, let the nymphs always sing to my ears the glory of your divine life."

SONGS OF NYMPHS IN THE AŚOKA GARDEN

It is stated in *Rām* (seventh *kāṇḍa*) that once Rāmacandra had a chance to visit the Aśoka garden where Sītā had been kept a prisoner by Rāvaṇa after abduction. He heard the sweet songs of the beautiful *kinnara*s and nymphs, who were intoxicated with wine and adorned with jewels and ornaments. They began to regale Rāma with their songs and dancing.[95-96]

GANDHAKĀLĪ

Besides the *apsarase*s or nymphs described above, we find another *apsarā* who rose to eminence in Gandhakālī. Although she does not appear in the *Rām* of Vālmīki, yet she figures in the provincial works related to the story.[97]

Indrajit, the foremost and valiant son of Rāvaṇa, was slain by Lakṣmaṇa in battle. Wild in anger and revengeful Rāvaṇa attacked Lakṣmaṇa and pierced him with an invincible missile called *śaktiśela* and, thus, struck on the chest Lakṣmaṇa fell on the battlefield and became unconscious. Suṣena, the foremost physician and son of Dhanvantari, god of medicine, understood the gravity of the situation and devised a plan to have the necessary herbs, renowned as *viśalyakaraṇī*, found in the Gandhamādana mountain for his cure. Rāma accordingly passed the instruction of Suṣena and Hanumān went to bring the herbs during the night time itself as otherwise Lakṣmaṇa would succumb to his injuries.

But Rāvaṇa came to know of Rāma's plan. So in order to deceive Rāma he sent his maternal uncle Kālanemī, in the guise of a mendicant, to allure Hanumān to accept half his kingdom and give up his search for the herbs.

Kālanemī immediately proceeded towards that place and created an artificial garden and hermitage where he found

Hanumān. The hyprocritic sage invited Hanumān with humble words to pay a visit to his *āśrama*, to have rest and bathe in the pool nearby. Hanumān as a devotee of Rāma obliged to the proposal and descended into the lake. And no sooner had he plunged into the water, a she-crocodile hurriedly attacked Hanumān, who on his part lost no time and, immediately getting hold of the crocodile by her mouth, brought her to the bank. When he forcibly widened her jaws, the she-crocodile discarded her wretched form and transformed into a beautiful damsel. She disclosed that she was an *apsarā* Gandhakālī by name whose duty was to dance in the Court of gods, but as ill-luck would have it, she committed a wrong by touching the feet of Dakṣa while she was dancing. She was cursed by Dakṣa to transform into a she-crocodile, but after long prayer, she was consoled by the statement that after prolonged suffering she would be released by the touch of Hanumān, the true and faithful devotee of Lord Nārāyaṇa who would incarnate himself as Rāma in the house of Daśaratha in course of time. Gandhakālī also did not forget to warn Hanumān that the sage was none other than the deceitful Kālanemī who had been sent by Rāvaṇa, king of Laṅkā.

Thus saying Gandhakālī immediately flew to heaven.

CRITICAL APPRECIATION

From a perusal of legends of the *apsaras*es found in the *Rām* one may come to the conclusion that the *apsaras*es were born of water from which their name is derived. They were neither wedded to the gods nor to the *asura*s, and they are considered as concubines. Of course, Indra used their services to meet his narrow ends, particularly to seduce the seers and sages who undertook deep penance with a spiritual end in view.

Another important point to be noted is that their life was not always a 'bed' of roses; rather there were many ups and downs and imprecations were often hurled at them which affected their lives and sometimes resulted in tragic consequences.

One may note the instance of Rambhā and Rāvaṇa. Rambhā, although a courtesan, was betrothed to Nala-Kubera. It was a precedent they had set. But Rāvaṇa had violated the entreaties of Rambhā and raped her. As a result, Rāvaṇa invited a curse from Nala-Kubera which resulted in severe consequences for Rāvaṇa. It was like a warning for the generations to come.

Often the nymphs took part in dancing when greeting heroes of wars and this practice seems to have come down to us from time immemorial. Also they are found to have attended joyous moments like birth festivals and festivals commentary victory.

The *apsaras*es, being concubines, are similar to *devadāsīs* of temples in later periods.

The apsarases in the Mahābhārata

Although the great story of the Pāṇḍavas and Kauravas occupies a bulk of the great epic *Mbh*, numerous stories of the *apsaras*es also have contributed to the growth and development of the epic. A good number of sages and kings are found to have been born of *apsaras*es.

The *Mbh*[98] states that Kāśyapa married as many as thirteen daughters of Dakṣa, and Prādhā was one of them. She gave birth to a number of *apsaras*es named Alambuṣā, Miśrakeśī, Vidyutparṇā, Tilottamā, Aruṇā, Rakṣitā, Rambhā, Manoramā, Asitā, Subāhu, Subratā, Suratā, Supriyā Atibāhu and the *gandharvas*, Hāhā and Hūhū.

PRAMADVARĀ

In the Ādiparvan of the *Mbh*[99] there is a story retold by Ugraśarvā, a saint and the reciter of the *Mbh*, that Cyavana had a son Pramatī by name whose offspring was Ruru, a famous *ṛṣi* born of the union of Pramati and Ghṛtāci, an *apsarā* of famed beauty.

The Ādiparvan of the *Mbh*[100] mentions that the *apsarā* Pramadvarā was born of Menakā who had a chance to have intercourse with Viśvāvasu, the *gandharva* chief. After her birth the new-born baby was left lying near the *āśrama* of sage Sthūlakeśa, who out of tender love and affection brought her up with much care. In due course she became famous as Pramadvarā. She was married to Ruru, the son of Pramati and Ghṛtācī.

MATSYA AND SATYAVATĪ

The *Mbh*[101] says that Matsya (king) and Satyavatī were born of Adṛkā, an *apsarā* who lived in the river Yamunā in the form of a fish, as a result of her union with a sage. The story in brief runs as follows.

Once king Uparicara, a descendent of Purū, was hunting in the forest for a long while and he felt fervent lust for his wife who was living in the palace. He sent a bundle of semen through a hawk. But the hawk in her flight was chased by another bird. As a result the bundle fell from the beak of the carrier hawk the river Yamunā, where a great fish who was none other than Adṛkā, a cursed *apsarā*, devoured the bundle immediately, and she became pregnant in due time. She gave birth to two children which were found by a fisherman. They became renowned as Matsya, a king of later times, and Satyavatī, the girl-child brought up by the fisherman. Adṛkā got release from the curse of the sage in the long run. As the fragrance of her body was that of a fish, Satyavatī was at first known as Matsyagandhā. Later on she came to be called Satyavatī. Sage Parāśara happened to meet her and by the grace of the sage, she became Padmagandhā. As a result of her union with the sage she gave birth to the venerable sage Vyāsa who was also known as Kṛṣṇa Dvaipāyana.

MENAKĀ AND VIŚVĀMITRA

The story of Menakā and Viśvāmitra given in the *Rām* is mentioned in the *Mbh* as well. Menakā is categorised as the *daivika*, belonging to a divine class of the *apsarases*. Kālidāsa, the great poet, adapted the legend for re-shaping it to fit the form of a drama. This was his *Abhijñāna-Śākuntalam*.[102]

GAUTAMA AND JĀNAPADĪ

The *Mbh*[103] also describes a legend of Gautama's association with Jānapadī, an *apsarā*, as follows.

Once Gautama the honourable *ṛṣi* did penance to have immense power in archery and weapons. But Indra apprehending danger and afraid of losing his supremacy in the *devaloka*, sent Jānapadī to restrain Gautama from achieving his goal. Jānapadī went and stood before the *ṛṣi* and tried her best to seduce the seer, casting her glances with gesticulation.

In spite of doing hard penance, Gautama could not hold his patience at the lustful sight of Jānapadī whose garment could no longer conceal her amorous limbs. His eyes gleamed out of passion and his male-fluid fell amidst his arrows. As a result, in course of time, a twin of male and female children were born. A certain soldier of king Śāntanu, while he was chasing a deer, discovered the twin. Considering that them as offsprings of some powerful *ṛṣi*, he brought them to the capital and presented them to the king. The king conducted their social and ritual performance in due time. Gautama, who had left them in the forest previously, came there and shouldered the responsibility of teaching all the Śāstras to the male child Kṛpa. As a result Kṛpa grew up as an *astraguru* of the Kauravas and Pāṇḍavas and the daughter Kṛpī was given in marriage to Droṇācārya, the son of Bharadvāja.[104]

TILOTTAMĀ

The epic[105] also describes the great legend of Tilottamā, the famous *apsarā*. It may be assumed that she was created with a view to destroying the two gigantic demon brothers Sunda and Upasunda, who were most intimate to each other. They had a boon from Brahmā that they could not be defeated — unless and until a separation or differences between them broke their unity. Having obtained such invincible power from Brahmā, they began to terrorise the three worlds at their own will and power. At the fervent request of the gods Brahmā asked

Viśvakarman, the divine architect, to create a damsel with matchless beauty. Viśvakarman did accordingly and, as the very name indicates, she possesed such incomparable beauty that each and every small particle of her body was extraordinarily handsome, like little bits of beauty gathered from the jewels of the world. She was best among the beautiful female figures. Brahmā infused life in that beautiful body. She was sent to the twin brothers, each of whom demanded her as his spouse. They got wild in passion and started fighting with one another to have her. They both died in the fierce feud.

THE APSARASES IN THE DEVASABHKĀS

It is described that in the Court of Indra the *apsaras*es danced along with the *gandharvas*[106] and in the Court of Varuṇa they took part in dancing and singing in accompaniment to the music played by the *gandharvas*.[107]

THE APSARASES IN THE COURT OF KUBERA

It is said that Miśrakeśī, Rambhā, Citrasenā, Suṣmita, Cārunetrā, Ghṛtācī, Menakā, Puñjikasthalā, Viśvāca, Sahajanyā, Pramalocā, Urvaśī, Irā, Vargā, Saurabheyī, Śamicī, Budbudvā, Latā and such other thousands of *apsaras*es and *gandharvas* did propitiate and dance in the Court of Kubera.[108]

GHṚTĀCĪ AND THE SAGE BHARADVĀJA

Droṇācārya, who was known to be the *astraguru* of the famous Pāṇḍavas and the Kauravas, is said to have been born of the union of the venerable sage Bharadvāja and Ghṛtācī, a nymph. Once the sage had a chance to see the nymphs while he was proceeding to have bath in a pool. Ghṛtācī's cloth was blown by the wind, and at the sight of her, Bharadvāja could not resist his passion. His semen fell down but he did not leave it behind; rather he kept it in a pitcher (*droṇa*). In course of time a child was born from the pitcher. His name was Droṇa Bharadvāja. He brought him up and also taught him all the *śāstras* – enshrined in *vaidika* and *laukika* scriptures; he taught him especially the art of archery in later life. Droṇa was called *ayonisambhava*, born without womb.[109]

ARJUNA AND THE APSARASES

APSARASES IN THE BIRTH FESTIVAL OF ARJUNA

The *Mbh*[110] describes the activities of the *apsarases* during the birth festival of Arjuna, the third son of Kuntī. The large-eyed *apsarases* decked with ornaments who participated in the great festival were Anavadyā, Guṇamukhyā, Adṛkā, Somā, Miśrakeśī, Alambuṣā, Maricī, Śucikā, Vidyutparṇā, Asitā, Sabāhu, Tilottamā, Ambikā, Lakṣaṇā, Kṣemādevī, Rambhā, Manoramā, Supriyā, Gopālī, Puṇḍarikā, Sugandhā, Surasā, Pramathinī, Kāmyā, Śaradvatī, Menakā, Sahajanyā, Karṇikā, Puñjikasthalā, Ṛtusthalā, Ghṛtācī, Viśvācī, Pūrvacittī, Umalocā, and famous Pramalocā and Urvaśī. All these beautiful-eyed *apsarases* came down to the earth and sang on the occasion.

ARJUNA MEETS THE APSARESES

In another place the *Mbh*[111] states as to how Arjuna met the *apsarases*.

Arjuna went to Mahādeva Śiva in order to gain the Pāśupata missile at the advice of Vyāsa and the rest of his brothers. There he propitiated Mahādeva and gained the powerful missiles after long meditation and worship. Therefore, he was called by Indra, the chief of the gods, to visit the *svargaloka*. While Arjuna was proceeding towards *svargaloka* through the milky way he was enchanted by the music, song and dance of the celestial elves and fairies. Arjuna saw the Mandāra grove of Indra, under which the *apsarases* were engaged in sport and he delighted in the sweet-scented fragrance that issued out from the white lotuses and various kinds of flowers which touched his body. Then Arjuna was propitiated by the *apsarases* and the *gandharvas*. The band of *apsarases* consisted of Ghṛtācī, Menakā, Rambhā, Pūrvacittī, Svayamprabhā, Urvaśī, Miśrakeśī, Daṇḍagaurī, Varuthinī, Gopālī, Sahajanyā, Kumbhayoni, Prajāgarā,

Citrasesnā, Citralekhā, Svāhā, Madhusvarā, and other *apsarases* who were beautiful with eyes like lotuses in bloom and were employed in enticing the hearts of males with fair round hips and slim waists. They began to perform various dances shaking their heavy bosoms and casting their glances around, and exhibited other amorous attitudes capable of stealing the hearts of a resolute one.

VARGĀ AND ARJUNA

The *Mbh*[112] describes Arjuna meeting by chance an *apsarā* named Vargā. It is said that once Arjuna set out to travel all around the Bhāratvarṣa. In the course of his journey he saw a pool of water haunted by five *apsaras*es, in the form of five she-crocodiles. He was prohibited from proceeding towards the lake by the brāhmaṇas, but Arjuna being a dauntless valiant hero got into the pool and thereupon his feet were caught by a crocodile. Arjuna pulled her up to the bank and immediately the she-crocodile left her hideous form and transformed into a divine damsel. Arjuna was surprised to see her. The divine damsel told him of their past history: that they were the *apsaras* by name Sauraveyī, Śamicī, Budbudvā, Latā and Vargā, which was her own name. Once while they were trying to dissuade a sage from his hard penance, they were cursed by him to remain in the form of crocodile in that pool. After much prayer and propitiation, the sage granted them a boon that they would be released at the touch of a great person. Nārada too had felt sympathy for them and assured them that Arjuna, son of Kuntī, would release them from their wretched lives. Thereafter those five lakes were known as Agastya, Subhadrā, Paulamā, Karandhamā, and Śāpasenā respectively. Arjuna visited the rest of the lakes, released the cursed damsels and they returned to heaven.

It is also stated that king Yayāti made sportive with Viśvācī, a divine courtesan, in the delicate garden of Kubera.[113]

ABODE OF THE APSARASES

Moreover, it is mentioned in the *Mbh*[114] that the Sun God, *vasus*, *siddhas*, *marutas*, *gandharvas*, and the *apsarases* abide in the holy places of Puṣkara along with the apes. At the confluence of Kālikā, Kauśikī and Aruṇā (river), there lies the Urvaśī *tīrtha*.[122] And at Prabhāsa Viṣṇu resides along with the rivers and oceans. The *gandharvas*, the *apsarases*[115] and Prajāpati reside in that place. There was a splendid mountain which was the residence of the *gandharvas*, the *cāraṇas* and the *apsarases*[116] as also the *kirātas* and *kinnaras*. The famous Himālayas are said to be the abode of *apsarases* and *gandharvas*, as well as the *kinnaras*.[117]

A conversation that took place between Yudhiṣṭhira and the sage Lomaśa gives us a vivid picture of the place which was inhabited by the *kinnaras*, *apsarases*[118] and others. Moreover, the *gandharvan* is said to be the abode of the *ṛṣis*, the *siddhas*, and the *kinnaras*, and very favourable to the *gandharvas* and the *apsarases*.[119]

Numerous names of *apsarases* are mentioned in this work. They are Irā,[120] Umalocā,[121] Ṛtusthalā,[122] Karṇikā,[123] Kāmyā,[124] Kumbhayoni,[125] Keśinī,[126] Gaṇamukhyā,[127] Ghṛtācī,[128] Citralekhā,[129] Citrasenā,[130] Citrāṅgadā,[131] Viśvācī,[132] Jānapadī,[133] Tilottamā,[134] Puñjikasthalā,[135] Pramalocā,[136] Budbudvalatā,[137] Menakā,[138] Rambhā,[139] Lakṣaṇā,[140] Latā,[141] Vapu,[142] Vargā,[143] Vidyutparṇā,[144] Vidyutā,[145] Śāradvatī,[146] Śucikā,[147] Sahajanyā,[148] Sukeśī,[149] Samuktā,[150] Surajā,[151]and Suratā.[152]

It is also said that the divine *apsarases* were born taking the form of the sixteen thousand *gopīs* with whom Kṛṣṇa sported in the mortal world.

It is stated in the *Mbh*[153] that one day Mitra and Varuṇa happened to see the celestial beauty of Urvaśī on the seashore. They embraced Urvaśī and immediately the spirit of Vasiṣṭha entered the body of Urvaśī. After this Mitra and Varuṇa separated themselves from one another and assumed two different bodies. Varuṇa approached Urvaśī. Then fell his seminal fluid which was kept in a pot. She received the semen of Mitra in her womb; it had oozed out and fallen on the ground. She kept this fluid in the same pot along with that of Varuṇa. After a few days the pot broke open by itself, releasing two bodies of children who became renowned as Agastya and Vasiṣṭha in course of time. And further, it is described that Bharadvāja once fell in love with Ghṛtācī and his semen fell. As a result, a damsel by name Śravāvatī was born.[154]

Śukadeva is said to have been born out of the union of Vyāsa and Ghṛtācī.

Ghṛtācī is said to have exhibited her dance before Aṣṭāvakra (sage) in the Court of Kubera.

The apsarases in the Purāṇas

The *apsaras*es are described in almost all the Purāṇas as the nymphs of heaven — where Indra ruled. Their names signify a being 'moving in the water'.[155] They bear some similarity with Aphrodite of Greek mythology. Although they are less conspicuous in the Vedic literature, in the post-Vedic literature of India they figure prominently, particularly in the *Rām*[156] and *Mbh.*[157] In the previous sections we have seen how the activities of the *apsaras*es are described in the *Rām* and in the *Mbh.*[158] Now this section deals with the references to the *apsaras*es found in the Purāṇas. It will be seen as to how they influenced the lives of the *daitya*s and the *dānavas*.[159] As already noted, they also influenced the lives of seers and sages.[160]

There are numerous stories about the *apsaras*es in various Purāṇas. These Purāṇic accounts are now given below, according to the chronological order of the Purāṇas. According to some sources, the *Matsya* is at the head of the list of Purāṇas, and the *Skanda* is placed at the bottom, while some others place the *Vāyu* at the top of the list, showing the *Bhaviṣya* at the bottom. However, we are following the order as given by R.N. Dandekar.[161]

Among the eighteen great Purāṇas, the *VāP*[162] enumerates fourteen *apsarases*, the *HmvP*[163] ten. They are again distinguished[163] as *daivika* (divine) and *laukika* (worldly); the former are said to be ten in number and the latter thirty-four. These heavenly creatures are said to have fascinated heroes and deluded the mind of persons absorbed in penance, but in doing so some of them had to suffer from curses of lasting influence. Many romantic stories are included in the Epics and the Purāṇas, describing their illicit relations with mortals and immortals.

THE APSARASES IN THE VĀYU PURĀṆA

The *VāP*[164] enumerates the following *apsarases*, viz. Anavadyā, Aṇavasā, Aṇuvṛtā, Madhurapriyā, Arūpā, Subhayā and Bhāsī. They are said to have been born of Asitā, Manavatī, Sukeśī, daughters of Tamburu, Menakā, Sahajanyā Bhāminī, Puñjikasthalā Ghṛtasthalā, Ghṛtācī, Viśvācī, Urvī, Pravācī, Pramalocā and Anumalocā. These are prominent *apsarases* described in the *VāP*. This Purāṇa[165] has acknowledged that Urvaśī was born from the thigh of Nārāyaṇa, the supreme lord of the universe. So also does the *Vāmana Purāṇa*.[166]

THE APSARASES IN THE VIṢṆU PURĀṆA

It is said in the *ViṣP*[167] that Ghṛtācī and other divine nymphs danced before Lakṣmī when she rose from the churning ocean. The *ViṣP*[177] describes the Sun's movement in ascending order and descending during the *uttarāyaṇa* and *dakṣiṇāyaṇa* respectively. He is accompanied by a particular sage, a particular *gandharva*, a particular *apsarā*, a particular *yakṣa*, a particular serpent and a particular *rākṣasa*. They are said to have ruled over the chariot of the Sun for a period of a month. The following *apsarases* accompany *gandharvas*, the sages, the *yakṣas*, the serpents and the *rākṣasas* every month: nymph Kratusthalā in the month of Vaiśākha, Manu in the month of Jeṣtha, Sahajanyā in the month of Śrāvaṇa, Anumalocā in the month of Bhādra, Ghṛtācī in the month of Āśvina, Viśvācī in the month of Kārttika, Urvaśī in the month of Pauṣa, Tilottamā in the month of Māgha, and Rambhā in the month of Phālguna.

The *ViṣP*[168] also describes an episode which, in contrast to the account in the *Mbh*,[169] mentions Urvaśī as the mother of Kṛpa and Kṛpī.[170]

THE APSARASES IN THE BHĀGAVATA PURĀṆA

The *BhāgP*[171] mentions that during the churning of the milky ocean by the gods and the *asuras*, the *apsaras*es came out of the ocean. They were bedecked with pendants attached to their necklaces and clothes with colourful borders, and their movements were graceful. They captured the hearts of the residents of heaven by their bashful countenance, physical charms and playful demeanour.

THE APSARASES IN THE AGNI PURĀṆA AND GARUḌA PURĀṆA

In royal consecration, according to the *Agni Purāṇa*,[172] the *apsaras*es, who are known as divine damsels, are also invoked along with others. The name of the *apsaras*es who are invoked in the ceremony are Kūrūpā, Anavadyā, Sukeśī, Menakā, Sahajanyā, Kratuthalā, Ghṛtācī, Viśvācī, Puñjikathalā, Pramalocā, Urvaśī, Rambhā, Pañcacūḍā, Tilottamā, Citralekhā, Lakṣaṇā, and Varuṇī. The *GdP* also[173] mentions the same list.

THE APSARASES IN THE VĀMANA PURĀṆA

The *VāmP*[174] gives a detailed description of the origin of the *apsaras*es with the glorification of lord Keśava by the gods and the *gandharva*s. It is described that Nara and Nārāyaṇa underwent severe penance in the Badarīkāśrama and afraid of them, Indra sent Rambhā to provoke them. Along with her, he sent Kandarpa and the spring season to disturb their penance. Nārāyaṇa created Urvaśī from his thigh and Rambhā and her associates were astonished to see the matchless beauty of Urvaśī and Madana himself was startled to see her. The legend of the birth of Urvaśī from the thigh of Nārāyaṇa is described at length later in this work (chapter 4).

THE APSARASES IN THE PADMA PURĀṆA

The *PadmaP* states[175] that during the churning of the ocean, the *apsarases* were born along with some celestial things like Airāvata and lotus. Some scholars have opined that they were born of Muni.

THE APSARASES IN THE MĀRKAṆḌEYA PURĀṆA

It is described in the *MārkP*[176] that Nārada had a chance to visit the Indraloka, where he was to enjoy the songs and dances performed by the *gandharvas* and the *apsarases*. Nārada was received by Indra and he was asked to stay among Rambhā, Miśrakeśī, Tilottamā, Urvaśi, Ghr̥tācī and others, who were all foremost and famous for their dance and song. They were to entertain him with their performance. But instead, the nymphs began quarelling among themselves, each claiming her superiority over others. Indra asked Nārada to select the best of the *apsarases*. Nārada proposed that the *apsarā* who could disturb the austerity of Durvāsā, who was doing penance on the peak of a mountain, would be considered the best. Being afraid of Durvāsā, all of them hesitated to do so but an *apsarā* by name Vapastamā agreed to do it. Accordingly she went to that peak of the mountain where the sage was doing penance and started her enticing songs and dances. Durvāsā came to know of her motive and enraged, he cursed her to become a bird in the family of birds.

The Purāṇa[177] also states that in due course Vapastamā was born in the family of Kundana, the best of the birds, and later on became famous as Tārkṣa. Her mother was Madanikā, daughter of Menakā, and Rista had given birth to some *apsarases* who were associated with sun-worship.

THE APSARASES IN THE BRAHMAVAIVARTTA PURĀṆA

The *BrvP*[178] describes a legend of Ghr̥tācī (an *apsarā*) and Viśvakarman, the divine architect. Viśvakarman invited the *apsarā* for a union, but on refusal he cursed the *apsarā* to take birth as a low caste. In return Ghr̥tācī too cursed him to take birth in a low caste family. However, their union was achieved in the long run.

Moreover it is stated in the same Purāṇa[179] that once Rambhā fell in love with the venerable sage Devala, who did not reciprocate her love, and as a result Rambhā cursed him to have a crooked body. He became renowned as Aṣṭāvakra. In course of time, and at the touch of Rādhā and Kṛṣṇa, his deformed body became a normal one.

THE APSARASES IN THE BRAHMA AND MATSYA PURĀṆAS

The *BrP*[180] mentions that the *apsarases* were born of Muni and this is corroborated by the *MtP*.[181]

THE APSARASES IN THE HARIVAṀŚA PURĀṆA

The *HmvP* describes the *apsarases* as associates of the *gandharvas*. Their names are given as follows: Anavadyā, Anucā, Aruṇapriyā Aṇupā-sabhagā, Alambuṣā Miśrakeśī, Puṇḍarikā, Tilottamā, Surūpā, Lakṣaṇā, Kṣemā, Manoramā and Rambhā. All of them are said to be daughters of Prādhā.[182] It is said that with a view to increase the number of subjects these *apsarases* were created along with gods and birds, serpents, cows, and other beings.

But Menakā, Sahajanyā, Parhiṇī, Puñjikasthalā, Ghṛtasthalā, Ghṛtācī, Viśvācī, Urvaśī, Anumalocā, Pramalocā and Mānavatī are said to have been born of the mind of Prajāpati. They are known as *daivika* type of *apsarases*. Moreover, Citralekhā, a friend of Uṣā, daughter of Bāṇa, the demon king, of Śonitpur was originally an *apsarā*.[183]

THE APSARASES IN THE LIṄGA PURĀṆA

Just like the *VişP*,[184] the *Liṅga Purāṇa*[185] describes the role of the *apsarases* along with the *gandharvas* in the rotation of the Sun during the twelve months. The *apsarases* mentioned are as follows: Devīsalā Stalakūṭā, Sthalasukā, Subhaśreṇā, Sariṣṭā, Anumalocā, Ghṛtācī, Viśvācī, Urvaśī, Pūrvacittī, Tilottamā,

Rambhā and Ambhajanandā. They are said to have been born of Muni.

THE APSARASES IN THE KĀLIKĀ PURĀṆA

The *KāP*[186] says that Alambuṣā and other *apsaras*es were born of Prādhā. A list of their names is given.

THE APSARASES IN THE DEVĪ BHĀGAVATA

The *Devī Bhāgavata*,[187] a Upa-Purāṇa, gives a description of Urvaśī like the *Vāmana Purāṇa*. It also describes the birth story of Śuka and Matsyakanyā which may be an imitation of *Mbh* Ādiparvan.

Apsarases in the Kathā literature

The *Daśakumāracarita*,[188] a great romance of Daṇḍin, also throws light upon the role of the *apsaras*es. It will be useful to cite some examples from the work here.

(a) The fame which was possessed by Rājahaṁsa, the king of Puṣpapurī, is glorified as follows:

> He was rendered fragrant all around by great fame which was repeatedly praised by the youthful courtesans of heaven diverting themselves in the groves adjoining the suburbs of the capital of Indra.

(b) Reference of Tilottamā and Añjanā (Puñjikasthalā):

Instances of Tilottamā[189] and Añjanā[190] were referred to in the said work which shows its acquaintance with the *Rām* and the *Mbh*, and other post-Vedic works (Purāṇas).

(c) Apsarā Suratamañjarī:

It is said in that work that a silver chain enchained the ankles of Rājavāhana for two months, and suddenly fell from the prince's ankles. It assumed the form of an *apsarā*[191] who went round him keeping him to the right and with folded hands addressed him thus:

> I am an *apsarā* named Suratamañjarī, born of the rays of the Moon in the sky. Once a foolish swan mistook my face for a lotus and possessed it. I happened to fall on the head of the great sage Mārkaṇḍeya who had just emerged after having bathed in a lake of the Himālayas called Mandodaka. Incensed by the affront he hurled a curse upon me saying 'O wicked girl assume now a matallic form wherein your consciousness will be suspended.' Then being propitiated by me, he said that the calamity would end after I had served as fetters for your lotus feet for two months only, but my senses would not lose their powers.

APSARASES IN THE (HARṢACARITA)

The famous *HC* is a masterpiece of Bāṇabhaṭṭa. Historically it may be said to be a work of minimal value due to paucity of factual records and with reference to the description of Thāneśvar according to the poet. It may be called the land of the *apsarases*[192] for the lustful persons.

MAHĀŚVETĀ AS AN APSARĀ

It is described in the *Kādambarī* (a *Kathā*) of Bāṇabhaṭṭa that Mahāśvetā, a true companion of Kādambarī whom Candrapīḍa met all of a sudden, said that she was born of an *apsarā*, Gaurī by name with whom Haṁsa, the chief of the *gandharvas*, was entangled through marriage.[193]

The apsarases in the Kathā-sarit-sāgara

Somadeva, in his *Kathā-sarit-sāgara*[194] (*KSS*), describes the role of some *apsarases*, the prominent among whom are Alambuṣā, Tilottamā, Pramadvarā and Urvaśī.[195]

ALAMBUṢĀ

In the Kathāmukha of *KSS*[196] it is said that at the demise of

Satānīka, the grandson of Abhimanyu (son of Arjuna), Sahasrānīka ascended the throne left vacant by his father. He was summoned by Indra to attend a function held to celebrate the victory of the gods over the demons and in heaven, when Sahasrānīka saw the gods sporting with their females, he became unhappy. At this Indra said to him, O king do not be unhappy, your desire will be fulfilled. Your object of love in previous birth has been born on earth. Please hear the story about it. Once I, accompanied by a Vasu called Vidhūma, went to see Brahmā, while the latter was holding an assembly. At the same time there came Alambuṣā, an *apsarā*, to see Brahmā, when the wind took away her cloth baring her body. Vidhūma was overwhelmed by desire and the *apsarā* was also enamoured of him. Seeing their condition I, at the command of Brahmā, cursed both of you to take birth in the mortal world to fulfil your cherished desire. Thus, you, who was Vidhūma in the previous birth, have been born as Sahasrānīka and Alambuṣā has taken birth as Mṛgāvatī.

TILOTTAMA

When the king was returning from heaven with Mātali, Tilottamā saw him on his way home and asked him to wait for a while, but as Sahasrānīka's mind was deeply preoccupied with the thought of Alambuṣā, he did not hear her words. Being enraged she imprecated him thus,

> O king you are pining deeply out of love for one and have turned a deaf ear to my prayer. Therefore, you will have to suffer a prolonged separation from your wife lasting for fourteen years.[197]

RURŪ AND PRAMADVARĀ

In the KSS (2, 6, 76-78) the story of Rurū and Pramadvarā is described. In 2, 6, 77, it is said that Pramadvarā was begotten by Menakā and a vidyādhara.

References

1. Albert, C. Bourn, *A History of English Language*, Allied Publishers Private Ltd., Bombay, 1968, p. 23.

   Taraporewala, J.S., *The Element of Science of Language*, Cr, XII, p. 204.

   Banerjee, S.R., *A Handbook of Sanskrit Philosophy*, Calcutta, 1967.

2. Max Muller, *The Vedas*, Delhi, Varanasi, 1969.

   Barnnet, L.D., *Hindu Gods and Heroes*, Reprint, Delhi, 1977.

   Cox, G.U., *Mythology of the Aryan Nations*, Varanasi, 1963.

   Robert, V.M., *The Pelican History of the World*, p. 63.

3. Winternitz, M., *History of Indian Literature*, Part I, p. 3.
4. Lowice Spence, *Myths and Legends Series*, Germany Brachen Books, London, 1985, p. 59.
5. *Ibid.*, pp. 33-7.
6. John Pinsent, *Greek Mythology*, London, New York, Sydney, Toronto, 1969, p. 43.
7. *Ibid.*, 132-7.
8. *Ibid.*, p. 19.
9. *Ibid.*, p.117.
10. *Ibid.*, p 40.
11. Hervy, Sir Paul, *Greek Mythology*, pp. 40-3.
12. *Ibid.*, p. 63.
13. Henry Rasbtan, *Love of Nature Among Greeks and Romans*, George Harlarp Pvt. Ltd., London, Calcutta, Sydney, 1930, p. 86. John Pin Set *Greek Mythology*, p. 19.
14. "She is perhaps a neolithic fertility figure. Such as was to appear again and again as the embodiment of female equality. Later as Astarte and Aphrodite." *ibid.* 16, 18, 19, 22, 29, 30, 31, 33, 43, 53, 57, 79, 82, 117.
15. Winternitz, M., *A History of Indian Literature*, I, p. 118.

    Dange, S.A., *Sexual Symbolism from the Vedic Ritual*, Delhi, 1977, p. 67.

    Banerjee, Jetendranath, *The Development of Hindu Iconography*, C.U., Calcultta, 1956, p. 336.

    Banerjee, Prajesh, *Apsaras in Indian Dance*, New Delhi, 1982, p.13.

    Mani, Vettam, *Paurāṇic Encyclopaedia*, Delhi, Varanasi, 1974, p. 163.

    Banerjee, Prajesh has quoted Max Muller to support his view with reference to the *apsarases*.

    Ibid., pp. 10-12.

16. See Winternitz, M., *A History of Indian Literature*, New Delhi, vol. II (Buddhist *Jātaka*), p. 147. "Such symbolism is no longer mere provocative suggestions or allegory as in the Buddhist monuments of the Sanchi and Mathura Schools." Read also, Banerjee, P., *Apsarases in Indian Dance*, p. 11.

    "Popular Buddhism adopted the nymphs and the Mahavastu states that they were garlands of flowers and many jewels. They are also described in several of the *Jātaka* tales as one footed (Kakata Paadmiya), attaching importance to their nimble feet suited to dancing and attending on Sakka." (Pa, i.e. India) (Religious landmarks in Padakkatal Panzau, Tamil Culture and 1958, vol. VII, No, 4, p. 370).
17. Kanwar Lal, *Erotic Sculptures, A Study in Background*, Khajuraho, Erotic Sculpture, Khajuraho.

    Vajontaro, J., *Konark*, Publication Division, Ministry of Information Broadcasting, Govt. of India, p. 110.

    Also Banerjee, P., *Apsaras in Indian Dance*, pp. 80-96. Read also, Charles Fat, *Discovery of Indian Sculpture: A Brief History*, Affiliated East-West Press, New Delhi, 1970.

    In old India as in ancient Greece the masses of people do not seem to have taken great interest in the high gods of the priests; what they loved were the dear little lesser divinities like nymphs of all kinds and their male counterpart.
18. Read Bhāravi, *Apsarases in the Post Vedic Period* (Court Epics, ch.7).
19. 'Why the Erotic in Temple Architecture', *Mirror*, August, 1983, vol. XXVI, No. 10, Bombay, p. 66.
20. Winternitz, M., *A History of Indian Literature*, Vol. I, Part I, p. 117.
21. Dange, S.A., *Sexual Symbolism from the Vedic Ritual*, Ajanta Publication, 1974, pp. 58-9. Read also Banerjee, P., *Apsaras in Indian Dance*, p. 11.
22. Joshi, J.R., *Some Minor Divinities in Vedic Mythology*, Deccan College Post-Graduate and Research Institute, Poona, 1977, p. 156.
23. V.M. Hillyer and E.G. Hucy, *The Story of Sculpture, The Story of our Heritage*, Nelwon first published, Great Britain, 1967.
24. Banerjee, P., *Apsaras in Indian Dance*, p. 121.

    Kramrish Stella, *The Art of India through the Ages*, London, 1954.
25. Read *Amarakoṣa*, Chowkhamba Sanskrit Series, Varanasi 1, 1974, pp. 42-3.
26. Banerjee, P., *Apsaras in Indian Dance*, p.24.
27. *Ibid*.

28. Macdonell, A.A., *The Vedic Mythology*, 1972, p. 134.

Renou Luis, *Vedic India*, Indological Book House, Varanasi, p. 144.

Banarjee, Prajesh, *Apsaras in Indian Dance*, Cosmo Publication, Delhi, 1982, p. 9.

Ions Veranica, *Indian Mythology*, Paul Halye, London, 1967, pp. 68-9.

Winternitz, M., *A History of Indian Literature*, part-1 University of Calcutta, pp. 65-90.

Keith, A.B., *The Religion and Philosophy of the Veda*, London, 1925, pp. 182-4.

Wilkins, W.V., *Hindu Mythology*, Calcutta, Allahabad, 1973, pp. 383, 385.

29. *ṚV*, 7, 33, 9, 12, 9, 78, 3, 10, 123, 5; 136, 6.

30. Details of the legend are treated in the next chapter.

31. *ṚV*, 7, 33, 9:

tainninyām hṛdayasya preketaiḥ sahasravalśanabhihsam caranti ।
yamena tatam paridhim vayanto'psarasa upsedurvaṣiṣthāḥ ।।

32. *Ibid., ṚV*, 10, 123-5:

apsarā jarāmupasismiyāna
kośa bibhṛti parame vyoman ।
carata priyasya yanisu priyaḥ san
sidat pakṣe hiraṇyaye saivenaḥ ।।

ibid., The Hymns of the Ṛgveda, p. 630.

33. Read *ṚV*, 9, 78, 3:

samudriyā apsaraso maniṣīṇam

pāsīnā antarabhi somom akṣaraṇ ।

tā im hinvanti harmyasya sakṣanim

yācante sumnam pavamānam akṣitam ।।

34. *Ibid., ṚV*, 10, 136, 6.

39. *AV*, 4, 37, 2, 5; 6, 111, 4; 118, 1, 3; 130, 1; 7, 114, 3; 8, 5, 13; 9, 12, 10; 11, 11, 15; 12, 1, 13; 50, 14, 2; 9; 34; 35, etc.

40. Read *AV*, 2, 2, 1:

divyo gandharvo bhubanasya yaspatrekaeva nasmayo vikṣidyaḥ ।
tam tva yaumi brahmana divya deva namaste astu divi te sadhastham ।।

41. *Ibid.*, 2, 2, 3:

anavadyabhiḥ samujagma abhirapsarasvapi gandharva asit ।
samudra asam sadanam ma abhuyataḥ sadya a ca para ca yanti ।।

42. *Ibid.*, 2, 2, 4:

adhrye didyannakṣatriye ya viśvavasum gandharva sacadhve ।
tābhyo vo devir nama it kṛṇomi ।।

Vide '*sunbeams* are called the *apsarases* associated with the *gandharvas*'. It is occasionally accompanied by the epithet Viśvāvasu, 'possessing all goods'. Soma is further said to have dwelt among the *gandharvas* or to have been stolen by the *gandharva* Viśvāvasu.

43. *Ibid.*, 2, 2, 5:

yaḥ klandastamisicayo'ksakama manomuhaḥ ।
tabhyo gandharva patnibhyo'psarabhyo'karam numaḥ ।।

44. Macdonell, A.S., *History of Indian Literature*, pp. 8-9. Read also Bali, Suryakanta: *Historical and Critical Studies in the Atharvaveda*, 1981, p. 157.

45. Read *AV*, 4, 37, 4:

yatrasvattha nyagradha mahāvṛkṣaḥ śikharodinaḥ ।
tat pareta psarasaḥ pratibuddha abhutana ।।

"They are originally spirits of nature, river and forest deities. Rivers and trees are dwelling places in which they live only to entice mortals and injure them by unnatural co-habitation."

Winternitz, M., *A History of Indian Literature*, part I, p. 117.

46. Read, *AV*, 12, 1, 50ab:

ye gandharva apsaras ye carayaḥ kimidinaḥ ।

47. *Ibid.*, 4, 38, 1-4:

(a) *udvindantīm sañjayantīmpsarām sādhu devinīm* ।
glahe kṛtāni jṛnāhamāpsarām tāmiha huve ।।

(b) *vicanvatimākṛantīmpasarām sādhudevinām* ।
glahe kṛtani gṛham pśāratamiha huvi ।।

(c) *pariṇṛtyātyadadanā kṛtam glahāt* ।
sā naḥ kṛtāni susati prahāmapṇotu māyayā ।

(d) *yā akṣeṣu pramadante śucamakradham ca bibharti* ।
ānandinim pramodinamapsarām tāmiha huve ।। 4 ।।

48. Read *AV*, 4, 38, 5-7:

sūryasya raśminanu yāh sañcaranti marīcirvāyā anucañcaranti ।
yāsāmṛsabho durato vājinivānasadyah sarvāu lokān paryaiti rakṣan ।। 5 ।।

sa na etu homamimam juṣāṇo 'antiarikṣeṇa saha vājinīvānaḥ ।
antarikṣena saha vājinīvān kakīm vatsāmiha rakṣa vājin ।

ime te stokā bahulā chirbvāngiyante kekīmhate mano'stu ।

antarikṣena saha vājinīban kakini vatsāmiha rakṣa vajin ।
ava ghāso ayagraja iha vatsām nibadhimah yathānām va ismahe svāhā ।। 7 ।।

Ibid., *AV*, 4, 37, 2-7; 10-11:

nvā kayam apsaraso gandharvā cātayāmahe ।
ajaśṛṅgyaja rakṣaḥ sarvān gandhena nāśaya ।। 2 ।।

nadīm yantvampsarasopān tāramṛvāśvasam ।
gulgulu pilā nāla dyha kṣagandhiḥ pramgindani ।।

tat paretupsarasaḥ pratībuddhyābhutana ।। 3 ।।

yatraśvatthā nyagrodhā mahā vṛkṣaḥ śikhandinaḥ ।
tatparetapsarasaḥ pratibhaddhyā abhutana ।। 4 ।।

yatravaḥ prañkhyā haritā arjunāudt yatraghatā karkayah-saṁvadantī ।
tatparetapsarasaḥ pratibuddhyā abhutana ।। 5 ।।

trayamagannaṣadhinām vīrudhām vīryavatī ।

ajśṛṅgaya rātaku tikṣṇa śṛṅgi vṛsatu ।। 6 ।।

ānṛtyataḥ śikhandinā gandharva syāpsarāpateḥ ।
bhīnadsi muksāvapi yāmi śeṣaḥ ।। 7 ।।

avakādānabhiśācanapsu jytaya māmakān ।
piśacān sarvanoṣadherpramranīhi sahaśa ca ।। 10 ।।

śvevaikaḥ vaṣirivaikah kumāraḥ sarva keśakaḥ ।

priyo dṛśaiva bhūtvā gandharvaḥ sacare
strīya stamito nāsayāmasi brahman viyrauatā ।। 9 ।।

49. Read *AV*, 10, 9, 9:

devaḥpitaro manuṣya gandharvapsrasaśca ye ।
te tvā sarve gopsyantī sātirātram ati drava ।।

50. *Ibid*., 11, 6, 3: *ab*:

gandharva psaraso vrumah aśvina brahmanaspatim ।

51. *Ibid*., 12, 1, 50:

gandharvā apsaraso ye cārayaḥ kimīdinaḥ ।
piśācāt sarvā rakṣānsi tān āsmadbhume yāvaya ।।

52. *Ibid*., 12, 2, 9:

ye gandharva apsarasaḥ devareṣu vānaptayesu yadu tasthu ।

53. *Ibid*., 18,3, 23:

martāsaścidurvasīprakṛkṛn vrhe cid arya uparāsyayoḥ ।।

54. Read *YV*, 5.2:

agnejanitramasi vṛṣanau stha urvaśyāsyayurasi purūrava asi ।

gayatreṇa tvā chandayā manthāmi
traistuvhena tva chandasa manthami
ājatena tvā chandrasā manthāmi ।।

55. *Ibid*., 15, 15-19:

ayam puro harikeśaḥ sūryaraśmi stasya rathagṛtsacsa,

rathājacśa senānī grāmohyau

puñjikasthalā ca kratusthalā cāpsarasau, etc.

56. Under the above noted verses *YVS* 15, 15-19.
57. *Rām* 1, 45, 20-23.
58. Read *Rām* 1, 45, 33

apsunirmathanādeva rasattasmadvarastriyaḥ
utpetur manujasrostha tasmādapsaraso' bhavat.

59. *Ibid.*, 1, 45, 34

sasthikotya'bhavamstāsāmapsarā nām subacarsām ।
asankhyeyāstu kākutṣtha yā stansām paricārikāḥ ।।

60. *Ibid.*, 1, 45, 32-35

na tāḥ sma pratigr̥hnāuti sarve te devadānavāḥ
apratigrahanāttavai sarvāḥ sādhāranaḥ smr̥tāḥ ।।

61. *Ibid.*, 1, 5, 23, 32, 17, 24, 18, 17, 43, 32, 45, 32-35; 49, 19; 73, 63, 64, 11-12, 38, 76, 10, 2, 91, 16, 26, 45, 3, 11, 15; 16-19; 35, 16; 4, 24, 34, 40, 46, 41, 21, 43, 22, 46, 15, 6, 90, 75; 85, 107, 51, 128, 71, 7, 2, 9; 13-14; 11, 43, 26, 9, 29, 26, 31, 16, 69, 13, 16-21, 40, 106, 16, 110, 7, 141.
62. *Ibid.*, 1, 63.
63. Read *Rām* 1, 63, 4

tataḥ kālena mahatā manaka parampsarā ।
puskareṣu naraśreṣṭha snātam sanupācakrame ।।

tām dadraśa mahātejā mehakām kuśikatmajaḥ ।

rupenāpratimām tatra vidyutam jalade yathā ।।

kandarpadarpavaśagomunistāmidambrabit ।
apsaraḥ svāgatam testu vasa ceha mamāśrame ।।

anugrhniṣva bhadram te madanena vimahitam ।।

ityuktā sā varārohā tatra vāsanathakarot ।
tapasohi mahābigno viśvāmitramupugamat ।।

tasyām vasantyām varṣāni pañca pañca ca rāghava ।
viśvāmitrāśrame tasmin sukhena vyaticakramuḥ ।।

64. Read *Mbh.*, 1, 82-88 – 1, 86, 10, 16

janayamāsa sa munirplanakayam śakuntalām ।
pr̥ṣṭhe himavata ramye mālinimabhita nadīm ।।

......

nirjjane to vane yasmācśakuntaiḥ paribritā ।
śakuntaleti nāmāsyāḥ kr̥tāñcāpi tatamayā ।।

65. Read *Śak*, Kālidāsa, Act 1, p. 29:

gautamītīre purākila tasyā rājarṣerugratapasī vartamā
nasya kimapijātaśamdeva menaka nāmapsarāh presitā....

66. Read *Rām*, 1, 64, 11-12

sahasrāksaya tatkarma bijñāya munipaṅgavaḥ ।
rambhām krodha samāvistaḥ śaśāpa kuśikatmājaḥ ।।

67. *yanmām labhayase rambhe kāmakradhajayaiṣiṇam* ।
daśavarṣasahasrāni śailī sthāsyasi durbhage ।।

68. Read *Rām* 1, 73, 37:

divyadundubhinighaṣai gītavāditra niḥsvanaiḥ ।।

nanṛtuścāpsaraḥ sanghāḥ gandharvāśca jaguḥ phalam ।
vivāhe raghumukhyāntam tadadbhutamadṛśyata ।।

69. *Ibid.*, 1, 76, 10:

gandharvāpsarasaścaiva siddhacāraṇakinnrāḥ ।
yakṣarākṣasa-nāgāśca taddrastuṁ mahādbhutam ।।

70. *Ibid.*, 2, 91, 11-18.

71. *Ibid.*, 2, 91, 11-13.

72. *Ibid.*, 2, 91, 18.

ghṛtācīmatha viśvācī miśrakeśīmalabuṣam
nāgadattām ca hemām ca somamadṛkṛtasthalīm ।।

73. *Ibid.*, 3, 4, 16-8:

tumbura nāma gandharvaḥ śaptu vaiśravaneṇa hi ।

prasādyamanaśca māyā savvṛtnmām mahāyasāḥ ।

yadādāśarathī rāmastam vadhiṣyati saṅoyuge ।

tadā prakṛtimāphusvargam gamiṣyati ।

iti vaiśravaneṇa rājā rambhāsakta muvācaha ।।

74. *Ibid.*, 3, 11-21, 7:

idam pancāpsaro nāma tātakam sārvakālikam ।।

75. *Ibid.*, 4, 66, 8-9:

apsarānāma śreṣṭhā vikhyātā puñjikāsthalā
añjaneti parikhyātā patnī keśarinī hareḥ ।।

vikhyātā triṣu lakeṣa rupenāpratima bhuvi
abhiśapādabhutāt kapitve kāmarūpiṇī
duhitā vānarendra kuñjarasya mhātmanaḥ

76. *Ibid.*, 7, 35, 20:

tasya bhāryā babhubestā añajaneti pariśrutā ।

janayāmāsa tasyām bai vāyurātmajamuttama ।।

77. *Ibid.*, 4, 28, 51; 4, 29, 4-5.

78. *Ibid.*, 4, 35, 7:

ghṛtācyām killa saṅsktā daśavarṣāṇi lakṣmaṇa
aho 'manyata dharmātmā viśvāmitro mahāmuniḥ ।।

79. *Ibid.*, 1.32, 10

kuśanābhasta rājarṣiḥ kanyā śatamnusttamam ।
janāyāmāsa dharmātmā ghṛtācyām raghunandana ।।

80. *vivudhāścāraṇa yakṣāḥ kinnarāḥ sāpsaruganāḥ* ।
hṛstā samadhiganchanti nalinīm tām rirangsavaḥ ।

81. *Ibid.*, 4, 43, 21-22:

kuberabhavanam ramyam nirmitam viśvakrmaṇa ।।

viśālā nalinī yatra prabhutakamalotpalā ।
hansa kārandavākirnā hi apsaragnāsevitā ।।

82. *Rām*. 4, 43, 50:

striyaśca guṇasampannā rūpayauvanā lakṣitāḥ ।
gandharvāḥ kinnarāḥ siddhā nāgā vidyādhrāsthā ।।

ramante śatatam tatra nāribhiḥ bhāskaraprabhāḥ ।

83. S.R. Roy in his edition of the *Svapnavāsavadattā of Bhāsa* (p. 141) writes in this connection:

"A land of gods in the north of the Himālayas which as Tradition goes flows with milk and honey and abounds in beautiful nymphs", p. 141.

84. *Ibid.*, 4, 46, 15:

udayam tatra paśyāmi bibidhandramāu ।
kṣiradam sāgnam caiva nityampsarasālayam ।।

85. 4. 52, 27-28:

nimilayata cakṣanṣi sarve vānarapuṅgavaḥ ।
nahi niṣkramitaṁ śākyamanimīlitalacanaḥ ।।

Also 4. 5, 14-17

tamapsarasi homayām sakhīm dānavapuṅgavam

Also 4, 52-27-28:

mama priyasakhi hemānṛttagitaviśārada ।।
tayā dattavarā cāsmi rakṣāmi bhavanaivahat

86. The story in brief: Assamese version

When the two brothers Bhīma and Arjuna were in hunting beyond the river Godāvarī they had to spend one night in the forest. In the following morning they felt thirsty and moved hither and thither for water, and discovered a pool where to their utter surprise they saw a damsel who was very beautiful. She prayed to them earnestly to pull her out from the pool, but eventually both the brothers were dragged forcibly into the pool by the damsel. Then she disclosed her identity and said that she was wife of Mayadānava and her name was Hemā, an *apsarā*. She added that she was a captive of the great *dānava* Aśvakarṇa by name. On her advice both the Pāṇḍava brothers derived some invincible missiles from lord Viṣṇu. They killed the demon after a fierce battle and then returned with victory. Hemā was married to Arjuna in the long run.

87. Read *Rām* 7, 12-6-18:

hemānāmāpsarā tat śvatapūrvā, tvayā kanyā mandodarī nāma patnyārtha pratigṛyyatām ।।

See the note no. 85 also

88. *Ibid.*, 1, 10, 14:

ṛṣyaśṛṅga iti khyātam name karma ca mebhubi ।

cf. *Mbh*. 3, 110-380-95 (ch. 2, sec. 4).

see P. Banerjee *Apsaras in Indian Dance*, p. 83.

89. *Ibid.*, 3, 74-35:

apaśyatām tatastrata śarvaryā raṁyama śramam
yatra te sukṛtātmanu biharantī maharṣayah
tatpuṇyam savarī sthānam jagāmat samādhimā ।।

90. *Ibid.*, 7, 26-14-55.

91. *Ibid.*, 6, 60, 10.1:

seyam sītā mahābhāga jātā janakanandinī ।
umā nandiśvaraścāpi rambhā varuṇakanyakā ।।

92. Ibid., 6, 90, 86:

nṛttyādbhirapsarabhiśca gandharvaiśca mahātmābhi ।

and 6, 107, 81.

gandharvāpsarasām saṅghā dṛṣṭvā yuddhama upamam ।

93 *Ibid.*, 7, 2, 7:

tṛṇavindrāśramam gatvā hyyavasamunipuṅgava

94. *Ibid.*, 7, 11, 44:

tatradevāḥ sagandharvāḥ sāpsarouragakinnarāḥ
vihārasilām śatatam ramante sarvadāsṛtāḥ ।।

95. *Ibid.*, 7, 40, 17:ab:

yāvadrāma ka thā vīra cariṣyati mahitale ।

and 18 bc

tanmamāpasaraso rāma śrāvayeesnaraysabh ।।

96. *Ibid.*, 7, 42-20-21:

upāṇstyanśca rājānaṁ nṛtyagītaviśāradāḥ ।
vālāśca rapavatyaśca strīyaḥ pāna vaśanugāḥ ।।

97. See the *Rām* of Mādhava Kaṅdalī in Assamese 620-06:

sehi jalamāje pakhi grāhiveśa huyāthāka jalajanth bhuñjiyā apāra,
rāmakārya sādhivaka hanumanta yāivetathā, taikhānike mohar uddhāra ।।

see also *Rām* Kritivasa Baṅglā version 6, 42.

98. Read *Mbh.* 1, 60, 47-51:

prādhāhasutā mahābhagā devī dvarṣtāḥ purā ।। 47 ।।

alambuṣā miśrakeśī, vidyutparṇā tilottamā ।
aruṇā, rakṣitā caiva rambha tadvanmanoramā ।।

asitā ca subāhuśca suvratā suratā tathā
supriyā cātibahuścā bikhyātau ca hāhā hūhūḥ ।।

99. Read *ibid.*, 1, 7-2:

pramatistu rurū nāma ghṛtācyām samajijanat ।
rurū pramadvarāyāntu śunakam samajijanat ।।

100. *Ibid.*, 1, 7, 6:

atha apsarā menakā tasya tam garbham bhṛgunandena ut

101. *Ibid.*, 1, 57, 47:

tatrādṛketi bikhyātā brahmaśāpādvarapasarāḥ ।
mīnabhābamanuprāptā babhava yamunācari ।। 47 ।।

102. *Mbh.* 1, 65, 20-21:

tapyamānaḥ kila purā viśvāmitra mahāttapaḥ ।

subhṛśam tāpayāmāsa śakram suragaṇeśvaram ।। 20 ।।

bhītaḥ purandarastamanmenakāmidama brabrit ।। 21 ।।

103. *Ibid.*, 1, 114, 49-54:

tathaibāsarasa hṛstāḥ sarvālaṅkārabhūṣitā ।। 49 ।।

anunācānavadyā, ca guṇamukhyā gaṇavarā

adṛkā ca tathā samā miśrakeśī, alambuṣā ।। 50 ।।

marici śucikā caiva vidyutaparṇā tilottamā ।
ambikā lakṣaṇā, kṣemā devī rambhā manoramā ।। 51 ।।

asitā ca subāhuśca supriyā suvapustathā,
puṇḍarikā, sugandhā ca surasā ca pramāthini ।। 52 ।।

kāmyā śāradvatī caiva nanṛtustatra saṅghasaḥ ।
menakā sahajanyā ca paraṇikā puñjikasthalā ।। 53 ।।

krtusthalā ghṛtācī ca viśvācī pūrvacittiścāpi ।
umloceti ca bikhyātā pramloceti ca ta daśa ।।

urvaśīkādaśī tyeta jagurayātalocanāḥ ।। 54 ।।

104. *Ibid.*, 1, 129, 6, 11-20

see also V.S., Apte, *The Students Sanskrit-English Dictionary*, p. 161.

105. *Ibid.*, 1, 203, 11-17: Read especially verse 17:

tilam talam samāniya ratnanām yadvinirmitā ।
tilattameti tatatasyā nāma cakre pitāmahaḥ ।।

Legend of Sunda-Upasunda is described in *Mbh* 1, 203-4.

106. *Ibid.*, 1, 208, 9-21, 209, 1-24.

107. Read, *ibid.*, 2, 7-21

tathaivāpsarasa rājan gandharvaśca ।
nṛtyavāditragitaśahāsyiścah vividharapi ।।

108. *Ibid.*, 2, 9, 23:

gitavāditravantaśca gandharvāpsarsām gaṇāh ।
stuvanto varuṇam tasyām sarva eva samāsate ।।

109. *Ibid.*, 2, 10-12:

miśrakeśi, ca rambhāca citrasenā, sucismitā ।
cārunetrā ghṛtāci ca menakā puñjikasthalā ।।

viśvāci, sahajanyā ca pramlocā, urvaśī, irā ।
vargā ca saurabheyi ca samici vudvudā latā ।।

etaḥ sahasrāścanya nṛtyagītaviśāradāḥ ।
upatiṣṭhanti dhamadam pāṇḍava apsarasaṁgaṇaḥ ।।

110. *Ibid.*, 1, 154, 1-5.

111. *Ibid.*, 3, 44, 29-31

ghṛtāci menakā, rambhā, pūrvacitti svayamprabhā
urvaśī, miśrakeśi ca daṇḍagauri varuthinī ।। 29 ।।

gapāli sahajanyā ca kumbhayanī prajāgarā ।
citrasenā citralekhā sāhāca madhosvarā ।। 30 ।।

etāścānyāśca nanṛtus tatra varāṅganāḥ ।।

112. *viśvāśya sahitā rame bybhragahnadanevane* ।
alakāyām sa kālam to meruśṛṅge tavattare ।।

113. *Ibid.*, 3, 70-83.

ādityavasaśca rudrāḥ siddhaśca samamarudgaṇāḥ ।
gandharvapsarvasaścacaiva nityam samihihate ।।

114. *Ibid.*, 3, 82-135 ab:

urvaśī tirthamāsādya tataḥ somā śraman budhaḥ ।

115. *Ibid.*, 3, 83, 66-8

tathāgaccata rājendra prayesamṛṣi sanstatam saritaḥ
sagavaścaiva gandharvasarasā stathā
hariśca bhagavate ste prajāpate ।।

116. *Ibid.*, 3, 88, 17.

117. *Ibid.*, 3, 107, 7-10.

118. *Ibid.*, 3, 243, 6:

ṛṣisidhamārgatam gandharvapsaranām priyam ।
vivisuste mahātmanaḥ kinarcaritam girim ।।

117. *Ibid.*, 2, 10; 8, 3, 12, 11; 3, 140-223; 49, 96, 14

118. *Ibid.*, 1, 123, 60-65.
119. *Ibid.*, 1, 123, 60-68.
120. *Ibid.*, 1, 123, 60.
121. *Ibid.*, 1, 123, 60.
121 *Ibid.*, 3, 43, 30, 64-66.
122. *Ibid.*, 3, 43, 30.
123. *Ibid.*, 1, 123-61, 1, 65, 50.
124. *Ibid.*, 1, 122, 61.
125. *Ibid.*, 1, 21; 74, 1; 68; 1, 123, 64, 8, 1, 129, 65; 3, 43, 29, 2, 10, 10.
126. *Ibid.*, 3, 44, 10; 9, 34.
127. *Ibid.*, 2, 10-10, 3, 44, 10.
128. *Ibid.*, 3, 19-48, 13, 19-44.
129. *Ibid.*, 1, 123, 60.
130. *Ibid.*, 1, 129, 6, 1, 129, 11, 20.
131. *Ibid.*, 1, 65, 49, 210, 11, 14, 13, 141, 1.
132. *Ibid.*, 1, 123, 64, 2, 10, 10.
133. *Ibid.*, 1, 123, 69, 3, 10-10.
134. *Ibid.*, 2, 10, 9, 12, 1, 115, 10, 1, 116.
135. *Ibid.*, 1, 80, 69, 70, 2, 4-82, 112-64, 3, 43, 29.
136. *Ibid.*, 1, 65, 50, 1, 120, 62, 2, 10, 10, 3, 43-129, 3, 280, 60, 13.
137. *Ibid.*, 1, 123, 60.
138. *Ibid.*, 2, 10, 9, 12, 1, 215, 20, 23, 2, 216, 21.
139. *Ibid.*, 1, 22, 60, 65.
140. *Ibid.*, 1, 216, 7, 217, 35, 2, 10, 9, 12.
141. *Ibid.*, 1, 123, 60.
142. *Ibid.*, 1, 123, 60.
143. *Ibid.*, 1, 123, 60.
144. *Ibid.*, 1, 123, 64.
145. *Ibid.*, 1, 123, 62.
146. *Ibid.*, 1, 123, 64, 1, 74-68, 2, 10-10, 3, 43, 30.
147. *Ibid.*, 12, 19, 45.
148. *Ibid.*, 13, 19-45.
149. *Ibid.*, 1, 63, 1, 122, 63.
150 *Ibid.*, 12, 342-51-53.
151. *Ibid.*, 9, 48-65-66.
152. *Ibid.*, 12, 314-151, 2-10.

153. *Ibid.*, 13, 19-44.

154. Dowson, John, *Hindu Classical Dictionary*, Kegan Paul, 1928 pp. 19, 20

Walker, Bonjamin, *Hindu World*, vol. II M-2, George Allen and Unwin Ltd., 1988, pp. 143-4.

155. Pinsent, John, *Greek Mythology*, Paul Hanly London, New York, Sydney, Toronto, 1967, pp. 42-3.

156. *Rām.* 1, 45-20-22. See for details section on the *Rām.*

157. *Mbh.* 1, 60, 50-1-2. See for details section on the *Mbh.*

158. *Rām.* 1, 63. 3-24

(a) Viśvāmitra and Menakā

(b) Rāvaṇa and Rambhā, *Rām.* 7, 26. 24-46

(c) Mitrāvaruṇa and Urvaśī, *Rām.* 7, 56, 23-27

(d) Uparicara and Adṛkā, *Mbh.*

(e) Gautama and Jānapadā, *Mbh.* 1, 129-6-11-20

(f) Bharadvāja and Ghṛtācī, *Mbh.* 1, 129-35, 373, 43-29

159. *Mbh.* 1, 65-49, 2, 10, 10, 14.17, 211-19; *ibid.*, 3, 46-10, 22, 35, 46, 45, 50

160. *Mbh.* 3, 110-579.

161. Read, R.N. Dandekar, 'The Purāṇas', *The Cultural Heritage of India*, vol. II, p. 240.

162. Banerjee, P., *Apsaras in Indian Dance*, Cosmo Publications, New Delhi, 1982, p. 32; C.P. *VP*, 69.4, 7-34.

163. Read *HmV.* (Bhaviṣyat Parvan) 36-43-48-49.

menakā sahjanyā ca parṇikā, pramolocatisatadaśa.

164. Read *VāP*, 69, 46-51:

anavadyānanvasām ..... arūpām subhagām bhāsī urvaśyakadaśī smṛtāḥ

165. *VP*, 13, 69-51:

anadī nidhanasyathā yañjne nārāyaṇasya sa ।
urvoḥ sarvanavadyongi urvaśye kādasismṛtaḥ ।।

166. Read *VāP*, 7, 1-45-5.

167. Read *ViṣP*, 1, 9, 101-102.

168. *ViṣP*, 2, 10, 2-19.

Kratusthalā, Puñjikasthalā, Menakā, Rambhā, Sahajanyā, Pramalocā, Anumalocā, Ghṛtācī, Viśvācī, Urvaśī, Pūrvacittī, and Tillottamā are those *apsaras* presiding in zones of the Sun.

169. *ViṣP* 4, 19-65-68:

satyadhṛstsatu varapsarā mucarvaśīm dṛṣṭvā

retaḥ skannam śarastambepapāta ।।

taśca dvidhgatam patyadvayam kumāram kanyakā ca abhavat śāntanudṛṣṭvā kṛpayā jagrāha ।।

170. *Mbh.* 1.67, 7, 7-21:

yasturajonkṛpa nāma brahnarsi

Vide 1, 130-4:

tatahjānapadī nāma devakanyām sureśvara ।
tadadhijagmu sarvete dhanurvedam mahāratha ।।

171. Read *BhāgP*, 8, 8, 7:

tatascapsarasa jāta niṣka kanthya suvasasaḥ ।
ramaṇyaḥ svarginam valgugatilitavalokanaiḥ ।।

Read *AgP*, 219, 36-8:

pantu te kurūpamukhyā divyaścapsarasaṅganaḥ ।। 36 ।।

anavadyā, sukeśī ca menakā, sahajanyā ।
kratusthalā ghṛtācī ca viśvācī, puñjikasthalā ।। 37 ।।

pramalocā corvaśī rambhā pañcacūḍā tilottamā ।
citralekhā, lakṣaṇā ca puṇḍarikā ca varuṇī ।। 38 ।।

172. Read *GdP*, 1, 6, 52:

khagā ca yakṣarākṣānsi ..... manirapsarasastathā ।।

173. Read, *VāP*, 6, 2, 7:

sarve to devagandharva upagāyanti keśavam ।
tathaivapsarāsu hṛṣṭā sarvalaṅkāra bhūṣitā ।।

nanṛtaśca mahābhāga jagausayātalocanā ।
athaścaupsarasu-sahasraḥ ।।

174. See details in chapter 4.

See also *VāmP*, 7, 1, 4-5.

175. Read *PadmaP*, 3, 50-1:

manthane pārijāta ubhṛd decaśrindanadrumaḥ
rūpadāryaguṇapetastaścapsarasam guṇāḥ ।। 50 ।।

ṣaṣtikatayastadajata stamadeva dānavaiḥ
sarvanstaḥ kṛta pūrvastasamanya purvakarmana ।। 51 ।।

176. Read *MkP*, 1, 27-28, 30:

sakrasyapsarasamcaiva nāradasy ca sangame ।। 27 ।।

nārada nandaneapśyat puñscaliganamadhyagam ।
śakram surādhirajanam tan mukhasaktalocanām ।। 28 ।।

tam dṛṣṭvavanot valavṛtrajñamuthitam tridaśaṅganaḥ ।
pranemustaśca devarṣimbinyavantaḥ tgutaḥ ।। 30 ।।

See also verse 1, 32 and read 1, 41, 44 ff.

tatrapsarvapuamarnāma muniksobhana garbitam ।।
ityāktvā prajagamatha prāleadri mvapustada । etc.

177. *Ibid.*, 2, 30-32.

178. Read *Brahmavaivartta* P., 1, 10, 22 and 24:

katham deva viśvakarama viryadhanam cakara saḥ ।
sundrayamedhamayanca katham te patitastrayeh ।। 22 ।।

ghṛtācī kamataḥ kamam vesam cakre mañcharam ।
tam dadarśa viśvakarma gacchantīm puṣkarapathi ।। 24 ।।

179. *Ibid.*, 30, 59, 69, 101 and 107:

brahmiṣṭho devalo nāma kandarpa sama sundara ।। 59 ।।

tam dadarśa ha daivena rambhā sṛṅgāravallabhā ।।

atīva sundaram santam kandarpamiva sundaram ।। 68 ।।

ativavikṛtakaram triśulokeṣu garhitam ।। 101 ।।

astābraketi tannami kautukena mayakṛtam ।

sarvasmin pralaye naṣṭe ha madbhaktah pranaṣyati ।। 107 ।।

180. Read *BrP*, 2, 1, 10, only

tāsu devāḥ khagāḥ gavanagaditiyadānave ।
gandharvapsaraścaiva................ jātaḥ ।।

Also see 2, 1, 23-63.

181. Read *MtsP*, 6. 45.

munirmuninamaca ganam ganampsara sam tathā ।
tathakinnaragandharvana ristajanay advahun ।। 45 ।।

182. Read *HmV*, 6, 46:

tāsu devāḥ khagāḥ gavonāga ditijadanavaḥ ।
gandharvapsaraśaiva jagnire' anyaśca jatayaḥ ।। 48 ।।

Also read verses not found in critical edition published from BORI, Pune.

imāścapsārasaḥ puṇyā vividhaḥ punyalakṣaṇaḥ ।
susubhestau mahābhāga prādhā devarṣīpujitā ।।

anavadyā manukam ca abya nāma aruṇapriyam ।
anugām subhagām bhāsīm striyah prādhavya jayata ।।

alambuṣā miśrakeśī, puṇḍarikā, tillottamā ।
surūpā lakṣaṇā kṣemā, tathā rambhā, manoramā ।।

asitā ca subahuśca, subṛtā, sumukhi tathā ।
supriyā ca sugandhā ca surasā ca pramāthinī ।।

kāmyā śāradvatī mauniya pasaras smṛtā ।
viśvavasu bharanya ca gandharva caiva viśrūta ।।

menakā, sahajanyā ca parṇikā puñjikasthalā ।

ghṛtasthalā, ghṛtācī ca viśvācī, cārubhāsī tathā ।
amlocetikhya pramloceti cactadaśa ।
mānavatī capitatha vaidikapsaras tathā ॥
prajapatista sankalpa sambhūta bhuvanapriyā ॥

183. *Ibid.*, 127, 2-4-6, 128-49 (not found Pune edition).

tatasta divyarūpeṇa citralekhā varāpsarā ।
bhavan prasadyamasa devi ca prahasattadā ॥
prasadyantimasanam prahasan tapasayancha ।

184. Vis. 2, 10, 19 (see Note No. 168 above)

185. Read *LiṅgaP*, 36, 22, 37, 32-34:

gandharvapsarā bhisca gramam sarparaksasah ।
pradipayan sahasran suragatah pristhatu pyadhayaḥ ॥
menaka, sahajanyā ca pramlocaathā sasmitā ।
anumlocā ghṛtācī ca viśvācī covarśī tatha ॥

186. Read *KP*, 34, 81-82 (Sṛṣṭivicāra)

prādhāsutamahābhāgā devidevaṣisusattamā ।
alambuṣā, miśrakeśī, samicīścā manoramā ॥
vidyutparṇā rambhahyarana rakṣita tatha ।
subāhuh surata caivamuraja supriya tatha ।
vapustilottamā catimukhyā apsaraḥ smṛtāḥ ॥

187. Read *DevīBhāg* 1, 13, 1-33

sudamne tu divamyate rājyam cakre purūravas ।
.... srutvā urvaśī vasibhata cakametam maradhipam ॥

Vide 1, 14, 1-20 (for the description of Śuka's birth legend).

Vide 2, 1, 11-38 (for the description of Matsagandhyā).

Also vide 6, 1, 40-48.

188. Read Dkc. 1:

purandarata purāṅgana vanabiharana parayanagivaranatarana ganikagona ॥

189. *Ibid.*, 2, *pitāmahasya tilottamābhilāsa.*

190. *Ibid.*, 2, *anilkṣya (māruta) keśarī kalatra samagama.*

191. *Ibid.*, *pūrvapiṭhikā.*

sa cainam can dralekhāesviḥ kacidapsararapiṇī ।
bhātvā padakṣiṇāmkṛtvā prāñjalivyajiniṅgapat
deva diyatamugraha hidra cittam
aham smi samarasmisambhavā suratamañjarī nāma surasundarī ॥

192. Read *HC* III:

apsarasaḥ puramiti kambhiḥ

193. Read *Kd.* Pūrvabhāga, pp. 467-70:

gandharvanam tu dakṣatamajat dvitaya sambhavam to deva kula dvyam jātam ।

bhagavate dvitiyeva gaurī garitinananahimakirana kiraṇabadatuvavaḥ kanyakā prasutā ।

sa to bhagavata makaraketuneva ratiḥ saratsamayeneva kamalinī hansena sanjujitā ।।

194. *KSS* 2, 1, 24-29, 32-38, 6, 76-86; 6, 77ff.

195. Legend of Urvaśī (3, 2, 1-31) is treated in chapter 4.

196. Read *KSS* 2, 1, 24-29:

sthtesvasmasu tatraiva viriñcim drastum psasraḥ ।
agadalambuṣā nāma vatavisramsitansukā ।।

tam dṛṣṭvaiva sa kāmasya vaśaṁ vasurapagamat ।
sapyasparā jhagityasittadurpa kṛstalocanā ।।

tadālokya mamapasyanumukham kamalasambhavaḥ ।
abhiprayam viditvasya tavaham saptavankrudha ।।

martyaloke 'avatarāstu yavayoravinitayoḥ ।
bhaviṣyasthaśca tatraiva yuvam bharyapatiti ।।

sa vasustvam samutpannaḥ sahasrānīka bhupate ।
śatānīkasya tanayo bhūṣṇam śaśinaḥ kule ।।

sapyapasara ayodhyāyām kṛtavarmā nṛpātamjā ।
jāta mṛgāvatī nāma sate bhāryā bhaviṣyati ।।

197. *Ibid.*, 2. 1, 32-38

gaścantam sapsarāḥ prītyā tamuvāca tilottamā ।
rajanvakṣami te kiñcitpratikṣasva mānagīti ।।

tadaśrutvaiva heyaya śatam dhyānmṛgavatim ।
tataḥ sa lajjitā kopattam śaspa tilottamā ।। etc.

Part II

Legend of Urvaśī and Purūravas

3

Legend of Urvaśī and Purūravas in Vedic Literature

THE legend of Purūravas and Urvaśī is interesting dialogue hymn[1] and for some scholars, appears to be a ballad[2] that bears the theme of dramatic element with secular and religious tone. The legend is first described in the dialogue of Purūravas and Urvaśī, ṚV 10, 95. Urvaśī first appears in the ṚV 7, 33[3] revealing her glory of motherhood and two famous holy seers, Agastya and Vasiṣṭha, are born to her. The legend described in the ṚV 7, 33, and in the *Rāmāyaṇa*[4] states as to how Mitra and Varuṇa got excited at the sight of Urvaśī. Some portion of their seeds were dropped in a pitcher and some outside the pitcher. It is said that Vasiṣṭha was born from the seeds which had fallen outside the pitcher when the gods sympathetically collected them on the leaf of a lotus flower. Agastya was born from the pitcher and, therefore, he was called Māna, Mahadarya and Kumbhayoni. In ṚV, 7, 33, 14,[5] it is said that Māna introduced Vasiṣṭha to Pratardas as their priest.

Thus, this legend covertly suggests that Urvaśī was the mother of two great seers, Agastya and Vasiṣṭha. The legend is described in the *Rāmāyaṇa* by Vālmīki.[6]

Let us quote Griffith's translation of relevant verses of the hymn (7, 33, 9-12) below to have a look into the legend of the common birth of Vasiṣṭha and Agastya.[7]

They with perceptions of the heart in secret
resort to that which spreads a thousand branches.

The *apsaras* brought hither the Vasiṣṭhas
wearing the vesture spun for them by Yama.[8]
A form of lustre springing from the lightning wast
thou, when Varuṇa and Mitra saw thee.

They one and only birth was then,
Vasiṣṭha when from thy stock
Agastya brought thee hither.[9]
Born of their love for Urvaśī, Vasiṣṭha
thou, priest, art son of Varuṇa and Mitra,
And as a fallen drop, in heavenly
fervour, all the gods laid thee on
a lotus-blossom.[10]

He, thinker, knower both of earth and
heaven, endowed with many a gift,
bestowing thousands,

Destined to wear the vesture spun by
Yama, sprang from *apsaras* to life,
Vasiṣṭha.[11]

The dialogue hymn of the *R̥V*, 10, 95

The legend of Purūravas and Urvaśī is one of the popular themes throughout the Vedic and post-Vedic literature. The same theme is repeatedly treated in classical and modern literature too. The first instance of this legend is seen in the R̥gvedic hymn, 10, 95, which is variously perceived by the modern scholars. Some say it is a *saṁvāda* hymn, some say it is an *ākhyāna* or narrative hymn, while still others call it a ballad. In fact, it is one of about twenty such hymns which are popularly termed as the *saṁvāda sūkta*s.

The Purūravas and Urvaśī *saṁvāda* (*R̥V*, 10, 95) contains 19 verses in all. The hymn begins abruptly in a pathetic note of separation and also ends abruptly, leaving the readers in an inquisitive mood to search for its antecedents and proper conclusion. Before entering into such an inquiry, however, let us first put below the translation of the hymn in our own words.

Let us presume here that Urvaśī had lived with Purūravas for sometime, but now she is on the verge of parting from him under some compulsions. Thus, Purūravas finds himself in a state of melancholy. He first addresses his beloved:

> O my dear wife, O fierce one please tarry a little, let us exchange words. As such thoughts as these of ours, if remain unspoken now will not bring joy at a later day. (1)

Urvaśī replies with a strong determination not to stay with him any longer:

> Of what use will these words of yours be for me. I am going away like the first of the dawns. O Purūravas, I ask, you go back to your home again. I have become like the wind which is hard to catch. (2)

But Purūravas tries to convince her by drawing her attention to what would be his plight as a result of the impeding state of separation. He entreats her with the two verses 3-4:[12]

> Like an arrow sent for glory from the quiver, or like race winning cows, winning hundreds, I cannot shine in the religious ritual of the heroes, the battle, unless I continue to be a strong hero. When the battle has spread no soldier is capable of perceiving war cries. (3)

> She, who gave her wealth and life to the husband's father, came whenever her lover desired for her; she could go from that adjoining house and reach her own home, in which she could find her pleasure, day and night, with his virile limbs. (4)

According to tradition this verse contains Urvaśī's words, which is accepted by C.K. Raja[13] also. But according to some other scholars it was addressed by Purūravas to Urvaśī. Still there are some who call it an interpolation.

Now Urvaśī says to Purūravas:

> Three times a day you have given me conjugal happiness with your virile limbs, and you gave me all desires in full without my asking for the same. Purūravas, I yielded to your will, so you become lord of my body, O hero.[14] (5)

There would have been a number of queens in the harem of the king, Purūravas, and among them Urvaśī was treated specially. She complains that Purūravas keeps her under his domination. To this Purūravas replies thus:

> Sujurvī, Śreṇī, Sumnāpi, Hradecakṣus, Granthinī, Caraṇyu, attendants like these move about as if they were carrying jewels and cosmetics for you; like cows that yield milk, they did serve you.[15] (6)

The interpretation of the verse cannot be ascertained. These may be words of Urvaśī also. But according to tradition these are words of Purūravas. Now Urvaśī appreciates the magnanimity of Purūravas:

> As he was born, the Divine Ladies sat around him and the Rivers singing their praises nurtured him well. The Gods nourished you, O Purūravas, for the sake of their great battle, for the slaughter of the enemies (*dasyus*).[16] (7)

In verse 3, Purūravas stated his plight: that he was unable to take part in the battle. Now Urvaśī reminds him that he was nourished by the gods, so that he might assist them in their fight with the demon enemies. Responding to her words Purūravas tries to clear his position:

> When I, a mortal man, approached as a friend, these immortal ladies laying aside their raiment, they were all frightened of me and ran away from me like a terrified snake, like mares yoked to a chariot.[17] (8)

> When, a mortal man, lived close to them, the immortal nymphs freely conversing (among them) they made their bodies shine like some water-birds, like the horses at play while feeding on grass.[18] (19)

> She who flashed like falling lightning bringing all that I desired from the watery region. You gave birth to a valiant son. O Urvaśī may you pass through a long span of life.[19] (10)

Above we have a description of the happy and free life enjoyed by Purūravas in company with the divine damsels, resulting in the birth of a heroic son through Urvaśī. He wanted Urvaśī to remain with him for a further period of time. Urvaśī, however, tries to clear her position in the next verse.

> You were born for the sake of offering protection on earth, O Purūravas and you lavished that power on me (resulting in the birth of a son). I warned you, knowing the consequence on that very day, but you did not heed me, why are you talking then in vain.[20] (11)

Urvaśī agreed to live with the king Purūravas till a son should be born. She warned Purūravas about the impending birth of a son as a result of unconstrained conjugal enjoyment with her. But Purūravas did not listen to her words. So she became pregnant and in course of time a son was born. When the condition was thus broken, Urvaśī had to depart heaven.

> When the son will be born and seek for his father like a crying child he will let his tears roll once he knows me. Who would be able to disunite the couple of one mind when they have a common heart, so long as the fire burns in the hearth of the parents-in-law.[21] (12)

The child is the bond of unity between husband and wife. Purūravas draws Urvaśī's attention to the factor that when a child is born he would be sorry at finding one of his parents gone. So she should stay back irrespective of violation of any terms and conditions as long as the fire established at home on the occasion of their marriage was burning. Now Urvaśī says:

> I will comfort him when he lets his tears roll down. Like any child, he will cry for the suspicious care of his mother. You have imposed a son on me and that I shall send over to you in time. You may retreat to your home. As you were thoughtless so you cannot get me back.[22] (13)

Thus, she explains her position. But Purūravas does not find a ground here for his consolation. He is vexed and becomes unhappy. When his pleadings fail to convince Urvaśī, he takes up a new line of approach which is expressed in the next verse:

> Your lover shall run away to a farthest region and shall never return. He shall lie in the lap of Nirṛti (i.e., Death), and then rapacious wolves shall devour him up.[23] (14)

The verses[26] run thus:

> I, as a member of the Vasiṣṭha family (or most beloved lover) make this appeal to Urvaśī who pervades the heaven and measures out the mid-region. May the gifts of good works remain with you. May you return. My heart burns.[27] (17)

According to some this verse is spoken by Purūravas. But it appears to be the speech of a poet belonging to the Vasiṣṭha family. If perchance the latter version is accepted, then the whole hymn — the presentation of the dialogue — should be attributed to a seer of the Vasiṣṭha family, which cannot be ruled out as Urvaśī is considered as the mother of Vasiṣṭha in the VIIth *Maṇḍala*. Now in the last verse, we find an appeal to Purūravas but it may be the words of Urvaśī. Here only the natural law is indicated.

> O Purūravas, the son of Ilā, thus tell you these gods : you are anyway a kinsman/friend of Death. Your offspring will offer oblations to the gods, and you will

> enjoy a life of felicity on the back of heaven.[28] (18)

The dialogue of Purūravas and Urvaśī as found in the *ṚV* begins all of a sudden and ends so suddenly that it does not inform us of the circumstances that led to the separation of the lover. The background of the hymn is given in the *ŚB*. The Brāhmaṇic legend unfolds the very terms and conditions and also the circumstances under which Purūravas and Urvaśī parted each other's company.

The very old myth[29] of Purūravas and Urvaśī occupies a prominent place in the *ṚV* amongst the dialogue hymns[30] (*saṁvādas*), also called the *ākhyāna* hymns by H. Oldenberg.[31] Thus, the legend has reappeared once again in the *Śatapatha Brāhmaṇa*[32] as follows:

> (1) The nymph Urvaśī loved Purūravas, the son of Ilā. When she wedded him, she said, "Thrice a day shall thou embrace me, but do not lie with me against my will, and let me not see thee naked, for such is the way to behave with us, women."
>
> (2) She then dwelt with him for a long time, and was even with child of him, so long did she dwell with him. The *gandharvas* said to one another. "For a long time indeed has this Urvaśī dwelt among men. Devise some means of making her come back to us. Now take away one of the two lambs tied to her couch." The *gandharvas* then carried off one of the lambs.
>
> (3) "Alas," she cried "they are taking away my darling as if I were, where there is no hero and no man." They carried off the second; she spoke in the self-same manner.
>
> (4) He then thought within himself. "How can that (place) be without a hero, without a man, where I am." And naked as he was, he sprang after them and it was very long before he deemed it necessary to put on his

garment. Then the *gandharvas* produced a flash of lightning and she beheld him naked; even as by daylight. Then indeed she vanished. Here I am back, he said. She had vanished wailing with sorrow. He wandered all over Kurukṣetra. There was a lotus lake Antyaplakṣa where she was swimming about in the shape of a swan. (The nymphs were swimming about in the shape of swans.)

(5) And she (Urvaśī) recognising him said, "This is the man with whom I have dwelt." Then they said, "Let us appear to him." "So it be," she replied and they appeared to him.

(6) He then recognised her and implored her (*R̥V*, 10-95): "My wife, stay. Thou cruel of in mind. Let us now exchange words. If those remain untold as secrets of our heart it will not bring us joy in days to come." Stop, pray let us speak together — this is what he meant to say to her.

(7) She replied, (10. 95-2) "What concern have I with you to speak to thee. I have passed away like the first of the Dawns. Purūravas, go home again. I am like the wind, difficult to catch. Am I for thee, Go to home again".

(8) He then said to her in a sorrowful manner (10.95-14), "Then will die your friend. He will never come back, wolves will devour him. He will lie on Nirr̥ti's lap. The friend will either hang himself or the wolves will devour him."

(9) (*R̥V*, 10, 93-16) When changed in form she walked among mortals ate little ghee once a day and even then she felt satisfied therewith, she said.

Then the discourse in eighteen verses (that follows) has been handed down by the Bahvṛcas. Her heart took pity on him.

She said, "Come here on the last night of the year. . . . " Then she would lie with him for one night and a son would be born to them. Accordingly he came there on the last night of the year.

She then said to him, "Tomorrow morning the *gandharvas* will grant them a boon, and then you must make thy choice." When they will ask you to choose for me, you will say, "Let me be one of yourselves". In the morning the *gandharvas* granted him a boon and he said, "Let me be one of yourselves".

There the *gandharvas* taught him a particular form of sacrifice, through which a mortal gets changed into a *gandharva*.

The legend of Purūravas and Urvaśī which has reappeared in the *Śatapatha Brāhmaṇa* ends in their union through the grace of the *gandharvas*. It may be supported with the opinion of Macdonell:[33]

> The *ŚB* (11. 5. 9) has raised the fable of this episode on the slender fibre of the Ṛgvedic story and has made it lively and of abiding interest.

Urvaśī and Purūravas in the YV

The popular legend of Purūravas and Urvaśī did not end in the *Ṛgveda* and in the *ŚB*, but it has reappeared in the *YV* with reference to the sacrificial form. The narrative runs as follows.

The Adhvaryu invokes Agni with the piece of wood forming the lower part of the firedrills in which the spark is produced by rapid friction. Thus, are explained the formulas with which fire twirling is performed at the same sacrifice in which two friction sticks are addressed as the pair of lovers. Purūravas and his beloved are already known to have brought forth Āyu. The priest takes the lower friction stick with the words:

> Birth place art thou of Agni

Ye are spring
Thou art Urvaśī
Thou art Agni
Thou art Purūravas.
I rub and churn thee
With the *triṣṭubh* metre
I rub and churn thee with the *jagati* metre.[34]

It may be added here that the above-mentioned ritualistic practice found in the *YV* has some affinity with the ritual of some other ancient peoples.[35] Moreover, this popular legend has flashed to some extent which may have reference to her[36] and the legend has also hinted at the classification of various sacrifices invented during the Vedic and Brāhmaṇic periods in India.[37]

Urvaśī: One of the female seers of the Vedic mantras

The most popular Ṛgvedic legend of Purūravas and Urvaśī is not only a dialogue hymn (*saṁvāda sūkta*) but it also conveys the message that Urvaśī is included among the Vedic seers of that period. Like the two wives of sage Yājñavalkya who had chanced to share their husband's possession during the Upaniṣadic period, Urvaśī also had a chance to have the legitimate share of a wife. It is, of course, a matter of pride that in the days of *Ṛgveda* women appear to have enjoyed greater freedom and equality. We hear of several women seers whose hymns are included and preserved in the *ṚV*, the earliest record of the Indo-Āryans. We have a list of twenty-seven such women seers called *brahmavādinīs* in the *Ṛgveda*. "Of them Aditi, Juhu, Indrāṇī, Saramā, Urvaśī, Rātrī and Sūryā can be called divine or semi-divine beings of mythological character."[38] In the *AV* some new names of female deities are found. Urvaśī is one of them.

We may remark in support of the opinion of noted scholars like M. Winternitz that during the Vedic age women enjoyed advantages in sacrificial jobs. It is also obvious that women of the three higher castes were invested with the sacred thread, allowed to utter the Sāvitrī verse, study the Vedas and take part in sacrifices with their husbands.[39]

It was reckoned as absolutely essential that the husband and wife together perform the sacred ceremonies.[40]

Urvaśī Purūravas: Ākhyāna theory

It goes without saying that people generally have a liking for direct speech in the narrative. Consequently the narrative came to be gradually dramatised, and verses began to be normally employed with a view to heightening interest or feeling. An instance of this is the dialogue of Purūravas and Urvaśī, which bears the germ of *ākhyāna* for the later period. As a consequence this type of legend, which is an admixture of prose and verse, became a source of epic poetry.[41]

The legend is an allegory

Max Muller,[42] in his selected essays, analyses the etymology of the words 'Urvaśī' and 'Purūravas' and proposes to think that they represented Uṣā or the Dawn and the sun. Purūravas presonifies the 'Sun' while Urvaśī is the 'morning mist'. Dr. Goldstücker has also made the same type of remark in this connection: "Urvaśī vanishes when the Sun shines forth and the mist is absorbed."

The dramatic element in the legend

Johan Hertel has tried to prove that the *saṁvāda sūkta*s were really speeches belonging to some dramatic performances connected with the religious cult.[42] L. Von Schroeder lends support to his view.[43]

Thus, the *saṁvāda sūkta* of Purūravas and Urvaśī which contains a dialogue is said to be one of the earliest forms of dramatic literature in India.

A love legend

The famous and popular legend of Purūravas and Urvaśī bears

not only the dramatic element, but also the theme of a love affair in Indian literature. Scholars like Macdonell are of strong opinion that this very old myth not only belongs to an Indo-European love story but also bears a long history in Indian literature.[44] This love legend is like 'an oasis in the desert'. This legend, which is one of the earliest Indian poems embodied with the passion and warmth of love, is a passionate expression of a mortal's love for a nymph; it has been retold in Indian literature by no less a poet than Kālidāsa who took it as the theme of his finest drama. This opinion has been supported with reference to the subject matter of *Vikramorvaśīyam* by some scholars with high praise.[45]

In the *Nir* 5, 13[46] Yāska derives the word Urvaśī as follows:

> Urvaśī is (the name of) a naiad, (so called because) she pervades wide regions (*urū+vas,* to pervade) or she pervades by means of thighs (*uru+vas,* to pervade) or her desire is great (*uru+vas,* to desire).[47]

Analysis of the word 'Urvaśī' and 'Purūravas'

The name 'Purūravas' signifies 'cloud'. 'Purūravas' he who excessively shouts like clouds and 'Urvaśī', 'lighting', with Urū meaning 'lustful', 'prevails much'. And as a result of the union of the couple Āyu was born. Āyu was none other than *anna* (food). Yāska also supports this remark and the definition and derivative meaning given in the *Yajurveda*.[48]

Urvaśī and Purūravas in Bṛhaddevatā

The popular and famous legend found in the *Ṛgveda* (10, 95) and *Śatapatha Brāhmaṇa* once again reappears in the *Bṛhaddevatā,* ascribed to Śaunaka. The story in brief is as follows:[49]

> Now in days of yore the nymph Urvaśī dwelt with the royal seer Purūravas and having made a compact (with him) had lived in wedlock with him.
>
> And the Chastiser of Pāka Indra being jealous of his

> co-habitation with her and of Brahmā's (*pitāmaha*) and his Purūravas's passion (for her) as if (Purūravas) were Indra.
>
> Said to the bolt at his side with a view to separating them, "Destroy O bolt, the alliance of these two, if you wish (to do) a favour."
>
> "Very well," said the bolt, and destroyed their alliance with its craft. Then bereft of her the king wandered about like one distracted.
>
> As he wandered, he saw in a lake the beautiful (*abhirūpam*) Urvaśī as it seemed surrounded by five beautiful maiden friends at her side.

This is the background of the hymn (*ṚV*, 10, 95) and the words of Purūravas followed by those of Urvaśī are given.

It is mentioned in the *Nirukta*[50] repeatedly that Vasiṣṭha and Agastya were born of Urvaśī.This has similarity with the narrative mentioned in the *Bṛhaddevatā*.[51]

Here we find introduction of Indra and his bolt to separate the alliance of the lovers.

Urvaśī and Purūravas in Nītimañjarī

The *Nītimañjarī*,[52] a later work, attempts at giving the legend in some detail on the basis of the original legend found in the *ṚV* (10, 95). The author has gathered almost all information which were current in the traditional sources and tried his best to synthesise them in his presentation of the legend. The description is found not only in the Ṛgvedic legend but also in the post-Vedic versions. The work consists of fifteen verses revealing the same traditional information as *joto mūḍho duḥkhamāpa purūravas*:[53] No man should be a slave of women, although he may be attached to her deeply and he should not be dull and if he be so, like Purūravas, he will suffer the pangs of separation.[54]

Urvaśī and Purūravas Vedārthadīpikā

The *Vedārthadīpikā*,[55] a commentary of Sadguruśiṣya on the Sarvānukramaṇī, has followed the legend of Purūravas and Urvaśī in brief. The legend bears no novelty; it is only an imitation of the Ṛgvedic legend. It is given below.

The king Purūravas, son of Budha and Ilā, was in love with Urvaśī. Urvaśī reminded him to carry out the terms and conditions which were narrated in the said Vedic work (*ṚV*, 10-95), particularly that he should guard her two pet lambs. While he enjoyed sexual happiness with Urvaśī, the *gandharvas* hatched a plan and stole the lambs from her chamber. Hearing them yell Purūravas rushed out without his cloth covering him and having seen him in the undressed state, Urvaśī went away citing breach of trust. The king wandered like a mad one. After a prolonged search he chanced to discover her in the Mānasa lake making sport with her friends.

The remaining part of the legend is the same as the oft-quoted Vedic legend.

Now it appears from the foregoing description of the legend that:

(1) The legend of Purūravas and Urvaśī is one of the oldest love legends which gained currency in the Vedic age, and each of the Vedic works had to take note of it.

(2) The background of it is found in the *ŚB*, while the Ṛgvedic *saṁvāda* presents the conversation that took place between the lovers at the time of their separation.

(3) The legend is further stretched into the post-Vedic and classical Sanskrit literature as a popular theme apt even for dramatic adaptation.

(4) Some elements of the story were changed in course of time.

(5) Historical importance of the legend cannot be denied nor exaggerated.

References

1. Read Keith, A.B., *The Sanskrit Drama*, p. 14.

   M. Winternitz, *History of Indian Literature*, Calcutta, 1962, pp. 88-93. Some Problems of Sanskrit Literature, Calcutta.

2. Read Tilak, Raghakul. *A Short History of English Poetry*, Prakash Book Depot., Bareilly, U.P., 1968, p. 24. The word 'ballad' is derived from Latin *ballare* which means 'to dance'. Originally a ballad was a song — sung to the accompaniment of dancing. The minstrel or the bard would sing the main parts and the dancers would sing the refrain or certain lines which were frequently repeated. Often it was a form of dialogue. Thus, the popular ballad had a story with the dramatic element.

3. The *ṚV*, 7.33, 14, is considered as the family hymn of the Vasiṣṭhas. Vide Velankar Family hymns of the family Mandalas *JBBRHS* 181942

4. *Rām* Vālmikī 7, 56-7.

5. Read *upainumadhavam sumanasyanana a vogacchati pratardo vasiṣṭhaḥ.*

6. *Rām*. 7, 56-7.

7. Hymns from the *Ṛgveda*, pp. 350-2.

8. Read *ṚV*, 10, 95, 1:

   haye jāye manasā tiṣṭha ghore bacāñsi miśkṛṇavavahai na noumantra. aṇaditā saḥ ete mayaḥ ksanau paratare can aham ।।

9. Read, *ṚV*, 10. 95, 2:

   kim etā bācā kṛnavā avā aham prākramisam
   usasam agriyaeva, purūrava punaharastam
   parachi durāpana vātaīva aham asmi ।।

10. Read *ṚV*, 10. 95, 3-4:

    eṣuh no śriye eṣuadha asnā goṣāh śata no raniḥ
    avīre kratau bida vidyuta no urā no māyam citayanta ahunnayah ।।

    sā vasu dhdhatī śvaśurāya vayaḥ uṣaḥyadi
    vasti antigṛhat astaṁ no nakṣeyasmiñ cā
    kandivā naktaṁ śnathitā vaitasena ।।

11. Quintessence of the *Ṛgveda*.

12. Read *ṚV*, 10. 95, 5:

    trihsma ma āhaḥ śrathalu vaitasena atasma
    mehavyantai puṇāsi purūravahana te ketam
    āyom rājā me vīra tanvahtatāsīh ।।

13. Read *ṚV*, 10, 95, 6:

    yāswagurṇih śreṇiḥ samnāpiḥ hṛdackṣaḥ

    na granthinī caraṇyaḥ tā añjayaḥ arunaḥ

na sasruḥ śriye gāvaḥ no dhenvahanavata.

14. Read R̥V, 10, 95, 7:

sam asmin jāyamāne āsam gnāḥ utaem
adrdhan nadyaḥ svagurtāḥ maheyatvā
prurūravaḥ raṇāya avadhayan-dasyhatyāyadevāḥ

15. Read, R̥V, 10, 95, 8:

sa cāyadāsa jahatīsu atkan amānuṣī so mānuṣa neṣeva apa smamat
tarasaretna bhjyaḥ taḥ atrasanarathasauti sprsaḥ naasvaḥ

16. Read, R̥V. 10, 95, 9:

yadāsa martaḥ amr̥tāsu niaspr̥ka sankṣhṇdi
bhiḥ krattabhiḥ na pratetaḥ ātāyaḥ no
tanvaḥ suṁbhūtaḥ svāḥ aścā saḥ no kr̥īldaiyaḥ dandaśānāḥ

17. Read, R̥V, 10, 95, 10:

vidyutr̥ṇāya patontī dāvdyut bharatī me apyākāmyā
hijaniṣṭa āpaḥ naṣyaḥ
sujātaḥ urvaśī tirata dirgham āyuḥ ।।

18. Read R̥V, 10, 95, 11:

jaugise itthā gapitthāya hi dadhāthatat
purūravas me ujarasāsasaṁ tvāviduṣī sasmin
aham no me a āsviṇah kim abhagavadāsi ।।

19. Read R̥V, 10, 95, 12:

kadāsunaḥ pitaraṁ jātahe isaḥ cākr̥an na aśra
vartyyan dijvñjū kah-dampate sa amanasā
bijijatadhayat agniḥ srvsra reṣudīdayat ।।

20 Read R̥V, 10, 95, 13:

prativravāṇi vartayate aścakran na krandatādheye śivāyani pratat te hinavā
yat te asmaḥ parachi astam nahimuramā āpaḥ ।।

21. Read R̥V, 10, 95, 14:

sudeva adya propteta anābrta parāvatam paramamgataḥ vai ahmadhī śayita
nihar̥terupsthe adhavr̥kāḥ ravasāsaḥ adyaḥ ।।

22. Read R̥V, 10, 95,15:

purūravaḥ mā mr̥thā mā proponaḥ mātvā vr̥kāsaḥ aśivāsaḥ am kṣaṇ na vai ।
straiṇāni sakhyāni santisālā vr̥kas hr̥dayani etām ।।

23. Read R̥V, 10, 95, 16:

yayadvirapā acanam mantedvasam rātrīḥ
śarada ctasrah gr̥hatasya stakaṁ sakr̥d ahaḥ
āśṇām ta eva dam tātr̥pāṇā carāmi ।।

24. Read R̥V, 10, 45, 17-18:

25. Read *ṚV*, 10, 95, 17:

    antakṣapārajasḥ vimānīmupa sikṣāmṛks
    urvaśī vasiṣṭha upatva rātriḥ sukṛtasya tiṣṭhān
    nivartasya hṛdayatapyate me । ।

26. Read *ṚV*, 10, 95, 18:

    ititvā devāḥ eme āhnella (aila) yathaim etatbhavasi
    mṛtyabandhaḥ, prajā te divān haviṣā yagti svarge enmtvam api mā dayāse । ।

27. Read *ṚV*, 1165, 170, 179, 3, 33, 4, 43, 10, 27, 28, 47, 48, 49, 50, 51, 52, 53, 86, 95, 108, 124.

28. *Ibid.*

29. Read Winternitz, M., *History of Indian Literature*, Part I, p. 182.

30. *Ibid.*, 88.

31. *Ibid.*, pp. 88-9.

    Read also Macdonell, A.A., *History of Sanskrit Literautre*, p. 183.

32. Read *ŚB* 5, 1, 1-9:

    Quoted by Narayan Ayyangar in his *Ancient Hindu Mythology*, New Delhi, p. 3. Quoted by Winternitz, M. in his *History of Indian Literature*, vol. I, Part I, p. 188.

33. Read Macdonell, A.A., *History of Sanskrit Literature*, p. 183:

    'The story of the love and separation of Purūravas and Urvaśī already dimly shadowed forth in a hymn of the *Ṛgveda* is here related with much more fulness.'

34. Read Winternitz, M., *History of Indian Literature*, vol. I, Part I, pp. 156-7.

35. *Ibid.*, p. 156.

36. *Ibid.*, p. 179.

37. Read Dange, S.A., *Sexual Symbolism from the Vedic Ritual*, pp. 187 and 203.

    Read also Dey, S. K., *Aspects of Sanskrit Literature*, Firma KLM Private Ltd, Calcutta, 1976, p. 178.

    Read also Basu Jagiraj, *India at the Age of the Brāhmaṇas*, Introduction I and p. 139.

    'The Kāmya or wish-yeilding sacrificer came under the occasional type. Wish-yeilding sacrifices are performed for the fulfilment of various desires of the sacrificer like the birth of sons and possession of wealth.'

38. 'Ghoṣā, Apālā and Yamī are some other women seers whose hymns are included in the *ṚV*. See Handique's *Women Poets of the Ṛgveda*, I.A. 50.

Read also Dey, S.K., *Aspects of Sanskrit Literature: Women Seers in the Vedic Literature*, p. 178.

Read also, Bali Suryakant, *Historical, Critical Studies in the Atharvaveda*, Nag Publishers, Delhi, 1981, p. 155.

39. Read Basu, Jagiraj, *India at the age of the Brāhmaṇas*, p. 214.

40. Read Winternitz, M., *History of Indian Literature*, vol. I, Part I, p. 57.

41. Read Shastri, P.S., *The Saṁvāda Sūkta of the Ṛgveda*, All India Oriental Conference, 13th Session, Nagpur University, 1946.

Read Bhat, G.K., A Thought on the Saṁvāda Sukta, *Journal of the University of Bombay*, vol. XXVIII, 1959, Part II, Sept. 1959.

Read Shastri, P.S., The Ṛgvedic Ballads, *The Poona Orientalist*, vol.X, No. 8, 3-4 July, 1945, Oct.

42. Maxmuller, *Myth and Reality*, 1868, Vol. II, pp. 117ff, p. 130.

Read Winternitz, M., *Ancient Indian Ballad Poetry: Some Problems of Indian Literature*, Calcutta University Readership lecture, 1929, p. 41.

43. Read Macdonell, A.A., *History of Sanskrit Literature*, p. 293.

Read also, 'The Dramatic Fragments of *Ṛgveda*', *Bharatiya Vidya*, vol. XVI, No. 2, 1956, Bombay.

Bhat, G.K., *JB* 32, Sep. 1957, vol. XXVI, 1958.

Die attindischo Akhyana in 2DM 39, pp. 52ff.

Winternitz, M., *History of Indian Literature*, vol. I, Part I, p. 89.

44. Read Macdonell, A.A., *History of Sanskrit Literature*, p. 183.

Ibid., p. 100 — "A good deal of interest attaches to this myth, not only as the oldest Indian European love-story but as one which had a long history in Indian Literature."

Read Winternitz, M., *History of Indian Literature*, Vol. I, Part I, p. 182.

Read also Dey, Susil Kumar, *Ancient Indian Erotic and Erotical Literature*, Firma K.L. Mukhapadhya, Calcutta, p. 1.

Also read Raj Chandella Umapali, *Hindī Sūfī Kāvya me Purāṇic Ākhyāna*, R.S. Chanhan, Ist Publication, Abinasa Prakasan, New Delhi, 1976, p. 40.

45. Read Macdonell, *History of Sanskrit Literature*, p. 183.

Read also Winternitz, M., *History of Indian Literature*, vol. I, Part I, p. 91.

Read also Bhaduri, Nrisingh Prasad, 'Purūravas ekajan gandharva haye galen.' *Mhābhārata Kathā*, *Bartaman* weekly, 4th Feb. 1955, Calcutta.

46. Read *Nir*, 5, 13, *urvaśyapsarā/urvabyasnute/urbhyām snute ururavā vasasyaḥ*

47. Sarup, L., *Nirukta* Jr. p. 81.
48. *Nir.* 5, 3.13.
49. Read *Bṛhaddevatā* VII, 140-7:

    tayurādityaḥ satre dṛṣṭvāpsaranurvaśīm retaṣkaṇḍaya
    tatkumbhe hypatdvasativare/
    janaivata muhurtena
    vriyanantou tapasvīnam agastyapśca vasiṣṭhaśca tasu sambhabhabataḥ ।।

    bahudhā patite śukre kalaṣatha jale sthale
    vasiṣṭhasta munih sambhata malsyamaha dyatiḥ ।।
50. See *Nirukta* 5, 3, 13.
51. See *ibid.*, p. 49.
52. Read Text Sridyadviveda racita Ed. by Sitaram Joyram Joshi, 1933.
53. *Ibid.*
54. *Ibid.*, 325-6-7-8.
55. *Ṛgvedic Sarvānukramaṇī Kātyāyana Anuvāka Śaunaka*, Dr. U.C. Sarmah, Viveka Publications, Aligarh, U.P.

4

The Legend of Urvaśī and Purūravas in the Post-Vedic Period

Urvaśī and Purūravas in Rāmāyaṇa

THE legend of Purūravas and Urvaśī is described not only in the Vedic works but also repeatedly in the Epic and Purāṇic works of post-Vedic literature. Vālmikī has, in the *Rāmāyaṇa*, given the legend which describes Urvaśī's association with Mitra and Varuṇa.[1] The legend runs as follows.

Once Nimi, of the Solar race, and Vasiṣṭha, a son of Brahmā, mutually hurled curses each on the other.[2] At the plea of Vasiṣṭha, Brahmā was pleased to grant a boon to him, that he might be reborn from the seed of Mitra and Varuṇa.[3]

Urvaśī, the chief of the *apsaras*es, along with her mates arrived at the house of Varuṇa at her will. Having seen her dance Varuṇa was overjoyed, and desired her company. But Urvaśī replied, saluting him with folded hands, "O lord of the gods, Mitradeva has already invited me." At this Varuṇa said to her that he would be satisfied only by discharging his seminal fluid in a pitcher. Urvaśī agreed to it. She said to him, "My mind is attached to you. You too are attached to me, but I am invited by Mitra already. So I shall have to abide by his call." Then Varuṇa deposited his semen in the pitcher.[4] When Urvaśī approached Mitra he was enraged at her and he said to Urvaśī, "O wicked one!

I had already contracted you, but avoiding me why did you attach to another. For this wickedness you shall have to go to the earth, to live with mortal Purūravas, the king of Kāśī, the son of Budha and he will be your husband." Saying so he also deposited his seed in the pitcher. Thus, being cursed by Mitra, Urvaśī was wedded to Purūravas, the king of Kāśī.[5]

It is said that from the semen deposited in the pitcher two seers, viz., Agastya and Vasiṣṭha were born. Urvaśī appears to be a symbol of the female who excited both Mitra and Varuṇa, and as a result of that Vasiṣṭha and Agastya were born from the seeds of the two gods.[6]

CRITICAL APPRECIATION

This legend of Urvaśī's association with Mitra and Varuṇa bears reference to the Ṛgvedic legend of the birth of Vasiṣṭha given in the VIIth *Maṇḍala* (7, 33).[7] This legend of the *Rām* may be treated as a commentary on the Ṛgvedic legend, particularly on verses 10-14. The *ṚV* legend of the birth of Vasiṣṭha and Agastya is found to be very obscure and enigmatic. The legend of the *Rām* throws light on it and with the help of it, one is capable of understanding the Ṛgvedic legend in a better way.[8]

Urvaśī and Purūravas in the Mahābhārata

In the *Mahābhārata*, Urvaśī's[9] name is mentioned frequently, especially along with that of other *apsaras*es, in her dancing attire.[10] But surprisingly one thing is to be noted: that the name of Purūravas is not mentioned in association with Urvaśī in the epic. However, Purūravas appears twice in the epic.[11] The epic narrates the story of Urvaśī and Purūravas as given below:

URVAŚĪ AND ṚṢYAŚṚṄGA

With reference to the birth story of Ṛṣyaśṛṅga, it is said that one day when the sage Bibhāṇḍaka was absorbed in deep mediation beside a lake, Urvaśī happened to be near him. He saw that an *apsarā* who was none other than Urvaśī was floating on the cloud. He could not resist his passion and as a result dropped his semen in the lake, where a doe was drinking water to quench her thirst. Consequently the doe conceived and gave birth to a human child who had a horn on his head, as his mother belonged to the ruminant genus. However, the doe was none other than an *apsarā* herself under the spell of a curse hurled upon her by a brāhmaṇa. Also the brāhmaṇa had predicted that she would be released from the curse when a sage would be born as her child.[4]

URVAŚĪ'S ROLE IN THE COURTS OF KUBERA AND INDRA

In the *Mbh*[13] Urvaśī along with a good number of *apsaras*es has been described as presenting dance and song in the Court of Kubera.[14] The names of the *apsaras*es include Miśrakeśī, Rambhā, Citrasenā, Suṣmitā, Cārunetrā, Ghṛtācī, Menakā, Puñjikasthalā, Viśvācī, Sahajanyā, Pramalocā, Irā, Vargā, Saurabheyī, Samicī and Vuda-vudvalatā. Further, the *Mbh*[15] has described how the *apsars*es headed by Urvaśī had exhibited dance that charmed the gods and the *siddha*s present in the Court of Indra. Her companions were as follows: Ghṛtācī, Miśrakeśī, Daṇḍagaurī, Varuthinī, Gopālī, Kambhayanī, Sahajanyā, Kambhani, Prajāgarā, Citraseṇā, Citralekhā, Svāhā and Madhusvarā.

URVAŚĪ AND ARJUNA IN THE INDRALOKA

In the Vanaparva[16] of the Epic *Mbh*, Urvaśī appears in a colourful manner. Following the advice of Indra, Urvaśī tries her best to seduce Arjuna, the third son of Pāṇḍu. The story runs as follows.

Once, when the five brothers of the Pāṇḍavas were living in the Dvaita forest in exile, being vanquished by the Kauravas in gambling, Yudhiṣṭhira sent Arjuna, at the advice of Vyāsa, to propitiate lord Śiva, with a view to acquiring divine missiles. Arjuna practised severe penance and pleased Śiva, who gave him the divine missiles. His father, Indra took him to Indraloka and made arrangements so that Arjuna might enjoy all sorts of pleasure in *svargaloka*. At the advice of Indra, Citrasena and Viśvāvasu directed Urvaśī to proceed to Arjuna so that the Pāṇḍava prince may enjoy her company. Being thus instructed, Urvaśī, the best of the *apsaras*es and the best of all in the female world, showing respect, agreed to the proposal and replied in a joyous mood.

Thereafter she rose, bathed and adorned herself with ornaments and divinely-scented garlands. In her imagination she dreamt of Arjuna lying with her, in a bed covered with celestial sheets. In the deepening twilight and early moonrise, she left for Arjuna's house. She wore clusters of flowers in her soft braids. Her delicate eyes gestured and her moon-rivalling face was shining brightly.

She arrived at the threshold of the chamber where Arjuna lived. Her arrival was reported by the doorkeeper to Arjuna. He asked the doorkeeper to usher her in as he himself apprehended fear in his mind. However, he came to greet her and saluted Urvaśī as a *śiṣya* or disciple does to a *guru*. Bowing his head in bashfulness, he said to her:

> I salute thee as a slave attends you.
> Please issue command as you like.[17]

Urvaśī, having heard the words of Arjuna, became perturbed, and she told what Citrasena, the chief of the *gandharva*s, had conveyed to her. She said,

> O the best of the persons. I have arrived here following the words of Citrasena. Please hear what happened, since your arrival in the heaven itself has adorned a garb of festival. The *rudras*, *ādityas*, *aśvinas* and the *vasus* have arrived here. So also the

> *siddhas*, *cāraṇas* (bards), *yakṣas*, great snakes, great seers, royal sages, effluent Agni, Iśānas, Bearer of Śaśa (Moon) have come to witness the festival. When they had taken their seats according to their seniority, music began following the sweet notes of the musical instruments and the principal *apsaras*es began to dance. Then you were seen gazing at me without a wink. At the end of the dance, the gods, *apsaras*es and others retired to their respective homes. After bidding adieu Indra sent Citrasena to me. Following the command of your father Citrasena said to me thus: 'O the beautiful one! I have come here by the order of the gods. You are asked to choose Pārtha, the valiant hero, as your husband. If you do so lord of the gods (Indra) and myself shall be pleased with you and your desire will also be satisfied.'[18]
>
> O the lotus eyed one! I have arrived here in order to serve you as directed by the lord of the gods, and the lord of the *gandharva*s. I am very fortunate as I have been pierced by the arrows of Cupid. Being charmed of your merits, I have arrived here. O the victor of enemies! You will be my master and this is my long-standing desire.

Hearing heard such kind words from Urvaśī, Arjuna felt exceedingly ashamed and placed his palms on his ears and said to her:

> O thoughtful one! This is quite an unbearable request to me. It would be unbecoming for me to agree to your prayer. You are like the wife of my *guru*. You are honourable to me as my mother Kuntī and Indrāṇī undoubtedly, O the auspicious one! Please listen to the cause of my taking interest in you. I was looking at you as the mother of the race of the Purūs. I should not be suspected as one with

> foul intention. O auspicious one! Did not the race of the Purūs originate from you? On that account you are my *guru*, adorable one.[19]

At this Urvaśī replied:

> O the son of lord of the gods. I am a common lady. It is improper to address me as a *guru*. The sons and the grandsons of the Purū race have spent much time enjoying me in their sport of love. They, after reaching the heaven by dint of merits acquired through penance, amused themselves by loving me. Please be kind enough to me and do not reject my prayer. Being afflicted with the arrows of Cupid I have become much attached to you, and request you to save my life by accepting me for enjoyment.[20]

Then Arjuna said to her:

> O the beautiful one! I am speaking the truth, please hear my words. Let all the lords of all directions hear my words. You are as honourable to me as Kuntī and Mādrī and Śacī are. O the faultless one! I do bow my head before you. You are worthy, honourable as any mother, and I am also to be protected as a son by you. Thus I pray to you kindly to return to your own abode.

Hearing such words from Arjuna, Urvaśī was angry with Arjuna, and raising her eyebrows and trembling, cursed him thus:

> O Pārtha! I have come to you being tormented by the arrows of Cupid and by the command of your father Indra. I came here as a female in search of love, yet you have rejected and discarded me. Therefore, I curse you that you shall have to spend some time as a eunuch,[21] the life of which is a disgraced one.

Having hurled the curse in that manner Urvaśī returned to her house after breathing a long sigh.

After her departure, Arjuna went to Citrasena, the lord of the *gandharvas*, and reported the incident that had occurred. He also added that he was cursed by the *apsarā* for disobeying her unholy request. Citrasena in return reported the incident to Indra who had directed Urvaśī to seduce Arjuna. Now Indra called on Arjuna and gave him solace, saying thus:

> O my son Pārtha! Today Kuntī bearing you as a son has proved worthwhile as you have surpassed the seers by virtue of your patience and self-control. The curse which has fallen on you will be a blessing in disguise for you. It will help you achieve a certain goal in course of time. O the faultless one! When you will have to remain in the forest *incognito*, during the thirteenth year, you will assume the form of a eunuch and being a dancer remain amidst the womenfolk and at the lapse of the year you will be able to regain manhood.[22]

The above-related legend has unfolded the following points:

1. Urvaśī was a common wife to be enjoyed by the gods and men freely. As she was not found to be in wedlock with Indra or Purūravas, she could share a bed with the descendants of Indra and Purūravas as well. Thus, when Indra sent Urvaśī to Arjuna he did not consider Urvaśī's relative position to Arjuna as Arjuna himself had perceived.

2. The legend brings out the best qualities of Arjuna. He is found to be an individual with considerable self-control. He was steadfast in his resolution not to touch a female who had shared the bed with his father or forefathers. However, he also neglected his duty towards a female who under passion had

approached him by failing to fulfil her desire. Thus, a curse hurled by Urvaśī caused him to suffer the punishment of becoming a eunuch for a year.

3. Another point may be noted and it is that the *Mbh* has deviated from the Ṛgvedic story and presented the story with novelty: a flaw of the flesh and blood is added to Urvaśī's personality. She finds no place in the reformed life of Indian womanhood, and her behaviour is rather reflected as a deteriorated one in the sexual life of the society where several kings, royal sages and men of reputation were found to be maligned.

URVAŚĪ AND ŚUKA

In another place in the said epic, Urvaśī is found approaching Śuka, the venerable sage. Once Śuka who maintained eternal celibacy amidst the prevailing sensuality is described to have rejected the prayer of Urvaśī. Urvaśī in utter surprise exclaims:

> O how wonderful is this youthful *dvija* full of intelligence and self-control who shines in the sky like a moon. The father must be very fond of such a brilliant son. How can his devoted father abandon him.[23]

Urvaśī and Purūravas in the Purāṇas

Like the *Rām* and the *Mbh* the Purāṇas also repeatedly describe the legend of Purūravas and Urvaśī.

URVAŚĪ AND PURŪRAVAS IN THE VĀYU PURĀṆA

The *VāP*[25] has described Purūravas as the son of Budha. Being attracted by his merits and personality Urvaśī married the king and spent long years indulging in worldly pleasure. Due to the curse of Brahmā on one occasion Urvaśī had to remain on earth. And it also said that Urvaśī made a contract with the king with three preconditions on the eve of their union.[26] With a view to breaking the contract the wicked *gandharvas* stole the rams in the dead of night from the bed-chamber of Urvaśī. Purūravas was seen naked by Urvaśī, while he attempted to rescue the rams from the clutches of the *gandharvas* and being enraged, she vanished immediately. After a prolonged search Purūravas discovered her and requested her to come back. Then Urvaśī consoled him thus: "Now I am pregnant". At the end of one year you will visit this very spot again and a son will be presented to you. Moreover, you will have the chance to spend a night with me. Thus, consoled Purūravas departed to his capital and obtained a son from her after a year. But having learnt of his ardent desire for her, Urvaśī advised him to worship the *gandharvas* and accordingly Purūravas was favoured by them. The couple were reunited for good in the long run.

The legend described in the *VāP* assumes no novelty, and it may be said to be of the ordinary type. But on the other hand, the Purāṇa introduced the curse of Brahmā which has similarity with that of Bharata found in Kālidāsa's *Vikramorvaśīyam*,[27] though the cause of the curse remains unspecified here.

URVAŚĪ AND PURŪRAVAS IN THE MATSYA PURĀṆA

The *MtP*[28] bears information as to Purūravas. It is said that Candramas had a son Budha by name. The latter had begotten a virtuous son in the womb of Iḍā or Ilā, and the son was known as Purūravas who had performed the *aśvamedha* sacrifice by dint of his power. One day he performed a holy *pūjā* in honour of Lord Janārdana[29] (Viṣṇu) in the splendid peak of the Himālayas and became lord of the seven islands and possessed immense wealth. He could drive away the demon Keśī and his mates in fierce battles several times.

Urvaśī was deeply captivated by his virtues and his personality. Through the grace of Viṣṇu he dealt in *dharma, artha, kāma* in a proper manner. Even it so happened one day that the three[30] (Dharma, Artha and Kāma) visited his Court to test his impartiality in worshipping them. He showed more respect to Dharma for which Artha and Kāma were offended. As a result they hurled curses on him to perish in no time. Kāma further said that he would be wild with pangs of separation from Urvaśī. However, Dharma had consoled him with the words:

> You will obtain longivity of life and be pious, and your descendants will rule on earth as long as the Sun and the Moon will shine upon the planet.

With these words he vanished in the air along with the others. One day while Purūravas was passing by the southern side of the land he saw that Urvaśī was forcibly being taken away by the demon, Keśī along with her intimate friend Citralekhā. He immediately pierced the demon with the *vāyavya* (windy) missile and released Urvaśī and her companion from his clutches and sent them to Indra. After this combat, there grew a mutual friendship between the king and god Indra. The gods also favoured him with immense wealth and power. In the meantime Bharata,[31] the revered and foremost expert in the *Nāṭyaśāstra*, produced a dramatic performance of the play entitled the *Lakṣmī-svayaṁvara*. Urvaśī and her mates were taking part in the performance. There Urvaśī, who had cherised a feeling of love towards the king in her heart, had a major role to play. As soon as the king arrived there as one of the audience Urvaśī committed an error in uttering her dialogue. She uttered the name of Purūravas instead of Puruṣottama as sought by Bharata. Thereby Bharata became enraged, and cursed Urvaśī to descend on the earth in the form of a creeper for about fifty and five thousand years, and at the same time he cursed the king to live in the form of a *piśāca*. At the end of the curse both of them would regain their original appearance and would be united. And, thus, they were united at the end of the curse in due time.

The *MtP* has deviated from the Vedic and Brāhmaṇic sources. It has omitted the terms and conditions which were mentioned in the original sources. The role of Dharma, Artha and Kāma is newly added. That Urvaśī would take the form of a creeper and Purūravas would take the form of a *piśāca* also may be assumed to be a novel creation. Perhaps this type of idea could appeal to the minds of the poets of the later period.

URVAŚĪ AND PURŪRAVAS IN THE VIṢṆU PURĀṆA

The legend of Purūravas and Urvaśī is given in the *VişP* as follows.

Purūravas was a very generous and famous donor and performer of numerous sacrifices. Due to the curse of Mitra and Varuṇa[32] when Urvaśī had to remain on the earth, she had a chance to have an interview with king Purūravas. Being charmed by his attractive personality, she was smitten with love and desired to unite with him discarding heavenly dignity and pleasure. She hurried to the king. The king was enchanted with her matchless beauty and, without hesitation, said:

"O lady of the beautiful thigh, I am attracted deeply to you and you too are attracted to me in the same manner." Discarding her womanly decorum, Urvaśī said in reply, "O king, if you are able to keep conditions then we may be united." The contract was that (1) Purūravas should guard the two lambs which belong to Urvaśī, (2) he should not be seen undressed except during intercourse, and (3) clarified butter should be supplied daily as her diet.[33] The king accepted all these conditions and promised her that he would keep his words and accordingly started roaming in the company of Urvaśī in intense joy. This way they spent sixty thousand years at various places. Being captivated with the worldly enjoyments, Urvaśī gave up all heavenly pleasure. However, her long absence in *svargaloka* made the *gandharva*s and *siddha*s among others think seriously of the ways and means to bring Urvaśī back to *svargaloka*.

Viśvāvasu, the chief of the *gandharva*s, thought of breaking the conditions of the contract of the loving couple. He made a plan with the help of the other *gandharva*s to bring Urvaśī back to heaven and accordingly, in the dead of night, they stole one of the rams from her chamber. The stolen ram yelled in fear. Hearing him yelling, Urvaśī cried aloud and said in utter despair and emotion, "Alas! I am helpless. Someone has stolen away my dear lambs. With whom shall I seek help for his recovery." And yet the king remained silent in fear of breaking the terms of the contract. Then the *gandharva*s stole the other ram speedily. Urvaśī cried out again out of anguish. The king being insulted hurried out in an undressed manner. But then the *gandharva*s put forth a flash of lightning upon him, so that Urvaśī could have a chance to see him in the naked condition. Having perceived the king so, which meant a violation of the terms of the contract, she vanished in a hurry.

The *gandharva*s left the rams, and the king having returned with those did not find Urvaśī in the apartment. He got wild in his pangs of separation and began to wander like a madman. He went in search of his beloved Urvaśī and at last discovered her sporting with some other *apsaras*es in a lake near Kurukṣetra. Bewildered and in utmost love, the king began to speak and prayed to her earnestly to return home. But Urvaśī said to him that she was pregnant with his child, and after a year their union would take place on the same spot.[34] She also added that he would be able to pass one night with her on the very spot. Being thus consoled, the king departed to his capital and after a year they were united on the very spot for a night.

Thus, Urvaśī presented him a son, and promised him that she would give birth to more offsprings in due time. Urvaśī learnt that the king was in grief owing to her long absence. The *gandharvas* being sympathetic offered him a firestick with the following advice.

> Initiating the gods you will divide Agni in three parts. Start a sacrifice with the intention of desiring the company of Urvaśī, then you will obtain your desired Urvaśī.

Having obtained the firesticks the king proceeded towards the capital, but on the way he left the firestick in the forest. When after a while he returned back to the spot, to his utter surprise, he discovered an *aśvattha* tree attached to a *śamī* tree instead of the firestick. He made up his mind to take the tree as the form of Agni and the oblations. He prepared *araṇī* worth of blazing fire. When he recited the *gāyatrī* meter *araṇī* produced fire adopting the number of syllables. Purūravas produced three kinds of fire through the help of *araṇī* and he offered oblations to the gods in fire desiring the company of Urvaśī. The *gandharvas* granted a boon to the king to become a *gandharva* himself and at last he was united with Urvaśī for good. In antiquity there was only one fire, but after the end of the *manvantara* Purūravas, grandson of Iḍā, produced three kinds of Agni, namely — *gārhapatya, dakṣiṇāgni* and *āhavanīya* respectively.[35]

The *VișP* does not deviate from the tradition of the Ṛgvedic and Brāhmaṇic (ŚPB) literature, but effects the slightest variation by describing Purūravas as a performer of sacrifices and as one given to charity. On the other hand, it adds the curse of Mitra-Varuṇa which may be assumed as an imitation of the *Rām* of Vālmīki.[36]

Urvaśī is shown as devoted to the king Purūravas as he was noble and charitable, but before acknowledging him as her husband she obliged him to agree to the three conditions which are in agreement with Vedic (*ṚV* 10-90) and Brāhmaṇic (ŚPB) legends. Purūravas, being captivated by her physical beauty, agreed to her proposal, but he failed in his task because of the conspiracy hatched by the *gandharvas*. As a result, he lost Urvaśī for a long period of time. His discovery of her near Kurukṣetra and their conversation in which Urvaśī says to him that she would present him a son after a year and he might spend a night with her then are novel to some extent. An addition to the legend which may be mentioned here is that Purūravas is found to be a devotee of Viṣṇu and it may be imagined that the cult of Viṣṇu became predominant at this time. Although the legend follows the original Vedic legend, yet four new points are added to the old story and they are as follows.

1. Invention of the *gandharvas*, advice to Purūravas to establish three fires and Purūravas' attainment of the boon that led him to be a *gandharva* are striking deviations from the original story.

2. Invention of two more fires in addition to the existent one is another point which is not met with in the Vedic legend.

3. Purūravas is depicted as a Vaiṣṇava here. In the *Kathā-sarit-sāgara* also he is presented as Vaiṣṇava. As the Purāṇa is a Vaiṣṇava one, it is but natural to depict the king as a devotee of Viṣṇu.

4. Urvaśī avows to present Purūravas with children. Indication that the king was probably sonless till that time is a new idea occurring in the Purāṇic legend here.

URVAŚĪ AND PURŪRAVAS IN THE BHĀGAVATA PURĀṆA

The *BhāgP*[37] also gives us details of the legend of Purūravas and Urvaśī. Purūravas was born of Budha in the womb of Iḍā or Ilā. He was a man of excessive power, and Nārada had praised his physical beauty and benevolence in the Court of Indra. Having heard his eulogy through Nārada, Urvaśī, the heavenly courtesan, was spellbound and was tormented by the arrows of cupid. Due to the curse of Mitra-Varuṇa,[38] she herself proceeded towards him and at her sight the eyes of the king danced in glee and emotion. Being thrilled in love for each other, they entered into a conversation. Urvaśī did not forget to tell him of the three conditions, which the king had to carry out sincerely. Nothing daunted the king, and he gave his consent to carry out the contract to his utmost ability. Once they were united in this way they made amorous sport in various places which increased their emotion deeply, and, thus, she spent a long period of time in worldly attachment. On the other hand, Indra, chief of the gods, felt the long absence of Urvaśī in the *svargaloka*. He pondered over it thus, "My Indraloka seems to be charmless in the absence of Urvaśī."[39] So he sent some *gandharvas* to bring Urvaśī back to *svargaloka*, and when the night was enveloped by a thick darkness, the *gandharvas* appeared in the abode of the king and stole the rams which were kept with care by Urvaśī. They began to bleat out of fear. Hearing them bleat, Urvaśī cried aloud, "O alas, I am falling at the hands of an irresponsible husband! He is a eunuch in the true sense of the term. I am undone enjoining on him. My pets are being stolen away by dacoits. He appears to be a hero outwardly but remains like a woman in slumber and in fear."[40] When Purūravas was taken to task in this way by Urvaśī, Purūravas rushed out in quest of the stolen rams in an undressed condition. The wicked *gandharvas* immediately put forth a flash of lightning upon the king, and Urvaśī chanced to see him in naked condition. She being enraged and offended vanished from the apartment. The *gandharvas* left the rams and the king returned with victory, but he did not find Urvaśī in the bed chamber. Bewildered and in pangs of separation he began to roam in search of his beloved Urvaśī. After a long search he discovered her at Sarasvatī lake near Kurukṣetra. Glad at heart, he started to deliver her a lecture in a passive mood. Adding thousand propitiations he caused fear in her by saying, "Let me loose to be devoured by the vultures and wolves." Then Urvaśī consoled him with the words:

> Let not the wolves devour you up. There is no everlasting love with women; their hearts are as hard as the hearts of wolves.[41]

> You will visit this place after a year. You will obtain one son after one year and we will have union between us for one night only.[42]

Purūravas came to know that Urvaśī was pregnant with a child in her womb and he returned back to his capital. After a year he revisited the place and found her there, spent one night with her and departed to the city. Having seen him in melancholy mood Urvaśī advised the king to propitiate the *gandharva*s so that they might be kind to him. At her advice Purūravas began to propitiate the *gandharva*s, and they being satisfied by his repeated prayers sympathised with him. They presented him with a fire vessel. The renowned king thought it to be Urvaśī and took it out but again decided to leave it in the forest. Then, at the advent of the *tretā yuga* (the thought of) three types of Agni were born in his heart (mind). He came back to the very spot where he had left the firesticks and to his utter surprise he discovered that an *aśvattha* tree had sprung up from the womb of the *śamī* tree. The king prepared two pieces of *araṇī* from the *aśvattha* tree with a desire to have Ụrvaśī and he placed the upper *araṇī* as Purūravas himself, and the middle portion was meditated upon as his son Āyu. Through churning of the stick Agni (fire) sprang up gradually, and, thus, three types of Agni were formed, which became renowned as *āhavanīya, dakṣiṇāgni* and *gārhaspatya* respectively. He also performed a sacrifice in honour of Viṣṇu with the hope of getting Urvaśī for a long time. But finally he could reconcile with his lot and he discarded the hope of regaining Urvaśī and also worldly love, realised the transitoriness of worldly love and pleasure, and meditated on lord Viṣṇu.

The *BhāgP* has made some innovations in the legend, where Nārada has a powerful role in bringing a union between the two lovers. Having heard the eulogy of the king Purūravas in the Court of Indra, Urvaśī was spellbound at the very outset and smitten with love she herself proceeded towards the king. She wanted to Court Purūravas as her husband before putting forth the preconditions. The *BhāgP* has not deviated from the Ṛgvedic and Brāhmaṇic legend on the major points. The conspiracy of the *gandharvas* to bring back Urvaśī to *svargaloka* is the same but in this Purāṇa the king's character is depicted as a henpecked husband, who has to bear all the insults of Urvaśī in coolness. Purūravas' propitiation could no longer influence the adamantine attitude of Urvaśī. And at last, he threatens Urvaśī that he would commit self-destruction with the following words: "Let me be devoured by the wolves" and in return her consolatory words are: "Let not the wolves devour you up and there is no everlasting love with women, their hearts are as hard as the hearts of wolves", which follows exactly the text of the legend as found in the *ṚV* 10, 95, 15-16:

> Do not die Purūravas nor perish, let not the evil predators and wolves devour thee. With women there can be no lasting friendship, hearts of hyenas are the hearts of women.

The last suggestive words of Urvaśī to the king that he should plead to the *gandharvas* for a lasting union with her is in imitation of the *Śatapatha Brāhmaṇa*, but his performance of a sacrifice to propitiate Viṣṇu throws new light on the introduction of the cult of Viṣṇu by that time. Purūravas becomes absorbed in the meditation of Viṣṇu as a result of the prevalence of the cult of Viṣṇu by that time.

URVAŚĪ AND PURŪRAVAS IN THE VĀMANA PURĀṆA

The *VāmP* gives us a detailed description of the birth story of Urvaśī. It is said that Nara and Nārāyaṇa were twin sons of Dharma, and they resorted to severe penance in the Badarikāśrama. Their penance alarmed Indra and other gods in heaven. Indra sent some *apsaras*es to dissuade Nara and Nārāyaṇa from continuing the penance. The Kandarpa with the host of *apsarās* and followed by his wife Rati and the vernal season (*vasanta*) appeared in the scene where Nara and Nārāyaṇa were absorbed in deep penance. But Nara and Nārāyaṇa who were omniscient came to know of their motive and asked them to take their seats beside them. They were utterly surprised to see that Nārāyaṇa, master of the three worlds, took a bough of mango flower in his hand and rubbed it on his thigh to create a damsel of exquisite beauty with golden limbs.

The bodyless Cupid, seeing the thigh-born damsel of matchless beauty, began to reflect within himself whether his wife Rati had appeared at that place. For it was the self-same charming face with beautiful eyes, the fine eyebrows, curly hair, attractive bridge of nose, and the lower hip the last resort, as it were, of the sense of sight. The very plump and thick breasts had sunk nipples in the close vicinity of each other after the manner of two gentlemen of one accord. The same soft and slender abdomen of the handsome damsel rendered charming by threefold of its skin and made beautiful with the line of hair appeared attractive.

The line of hair from the buttocks reaching to the slope of the breasts appeared as beautiful as a row of black bees from the bank of the lotus lake. The large buttocks decorated with the girdle appeared as graceful as the Mandāra mountain with the serpent (Vāsukī) going round it, on the occasion of the churning of the Milk Ocean.

The extremely handsome damsel, as a lotus filament, appeared graceful with her thighs which resembled plaintain trees with their roots outside. Her knees covered anklets charming hairless shanks and her left brilliant as the red the rendered her charming.

Then the sage exclaimed and said, "O Cupid! O *apsarases'* Mādhava! Take this damsel born of my thighs to heaven and present her to Indra."[44] Being, thus, commanded they proceeded tremblingly to heaven taking Urvaśī with them, and presented her to Indra as a gift of the sage Nārāyaṇa.[45]

Thus, the *VāmP* has invented a birth story of Urvaśī which is not found in any other work in Sanskrit literature. Her birth from the thighs (Urū) gives her the name Urvaśī. Besides, her presentation as a gift to Indra suggests that Indra was, thus, subjugated by Nārāyaṇa without much effort. The host of the *apsarases* and Mādhava were also ashamed of their mis-adventure and abstained themselves from such act against the two sages (Nara and Nārāyaṇa).

The story is repeated in the *DvP*, which is a later work, in the manner given below.

BIRTH STORY OF URVAŚĪ IN THE DEVĪ BHĀGAVATA

Like the *VāmP* the *DvP*[22] also narrates the birth story of Urvaśī in a colourful manner.

Nara and Nārāyaṇa, the famous twin sages, were in severe penance in the Badarīkāśrama when Indra, master of the gods, sent Cupid and his wife Rati with a troop of *apsarases* with a view to disturb their penance. Accordingly Cupid, his wife and the *apsarases* arrived in the penance grove and created an amorous situation, which changed the tranquil place immediately into a place of din and bustle. The songs of the birds, the sights and sounds of penance grove underwent a havoc change, and the self-controlled sages also failed to control their selves. Cupid entered the

Badarīkāśrama, where Rambhā, Tilottamā, and other *apsaras*es with dance and song started their passionate activities. The two sages were aroused. They heard the songs and saw the dance exhibited by the damsels and they began to ponder over the untimely advent of the spring season, which put them in a dilemma all of a sudden.

Then Nārāyaṇa looked at Nara with wonder and they had a talk with each other; they looked at the very spring season, which being decked with the flowers appeared charming, and heard the songs of the cuckoos. The forest had became splendid through the humming of the black bees. The bee-like spring season had shattered the winter season with the help of *palāśa* flowers which looked like the nails of a lion. They saw what wonderful beauty had appeared in the forest. The red *aśoka* flowers appeared as the hands of nature, the *kiṁśuka*s looked like her feet, the blue *aśoka* decorated her black hair, the newly bloomed lotus appeared as her beautiful face, the blue lotuses appeared as her two eyes, the *bilva* fruits appeared as her breasts. The *bandhujīva* flower was her own lip, *sindhuvāra*s seemed her nails, the sweet note of the cuckoo played as her sweet voice. The splendid *kadamba* flower seemed as her garment, the peacock appeared as her ornaments, the cackling sounds of swans were like the sound of her anklets, the *vāsantī* flower was as her girdle, the majestic walk of the swan was her movement, and the black hair of the *kadamba* appeared as her long braid.

They wondered why nature appeared so beautiful and untimely in this place. "She appears here to cause disturbance in our own penance. The celestial damsels sing and dance to disturb our minds. Indra, the lord of the gods, has made such preparation in order to destroy our austerity. Surely the killer of *asura*s is apprehensive and afraid of our austerity, and moves around heaven and earth to engage us in sensual thought. Otherwise why does the spring season appear so passionate and cause disturbance in our minds." Along with Cupid and his wife Rati, the *apsaras*es headed by Rambhā, Menakā, Tillotamā, Puṣpagandhā Sukeśī, Mahāśvetā, Manoramā, Pramadvarā, Ghṛtācī and others started their performance of dance and danced for a while. Then Nārāyaṇa created a damsel or *apsarā*, who ranked best among them, by suddenly rubbing his thigh. The damsel who sprang up from his thigh with exquisite beauty became renowned as Urvaśī. Seeing her matchless beauty and charm the rest of the *apsaras*es were badly frustrated. Cupid also began to see the unique beauty of Urvaśī created by Nārāyaṇa himself. Nārāyaṇa call upon Cupid to take her to heaven as a gift to Indra.

In a similar way the *Viṣṇudharmottara Purāṇa* speaks of the birth story of Urvaśī which is discussed later. The said Purāṇa gives a detailed description of the birth story of Vasiṣṭha and Agastya.

CRITICAL APPRECIATION OF THE VĀMANA AND THE DEVĪ PURĀṆA

The birth story of Urvaśī described in the *VāmP* is a new creation of the *purāṇakāra* in which his poetic fancy has found the fullest expression. And in appreciating the style and diction of the *DvP*, we may assume that it has affinity with the former. But the *VāmP* has omitted the love episode of Purūravas and Urvaśī, while the *DvP* has not failed to mention the said story in imitation of the other Purāṇas. The *DvP* also gives the birth story of Vasiṣṭha and Agastya, who were born through the union of Mitra and Varuṇa with Urvaśī.

URVAŚĪ AND PURŪRAVAS IN THE BRAHMA PURĀṆA

The *BrP*[47] describes Purūravas as one of the learned and best of the sons of Budha. He was mighty generous, fond of holding sacrifices and donor of ample *dakṣiṇā*s. He was also a *bramavādin*, knower of lores, valiant as well as destroyer of enemies. Urvaśī married him discarding her womanly dignity. The king spent a long period of ten thousand and sixty-seven years in the company of the celestial Urvaśī. He even roamed on the Citraratha to the bank of the river Mandākinī and in Alakā, and by far the best of the gardens of Nandana and reached Uttarakuru of the Gandhamādana hill on the peaks of the Meru mountain. The king wandered alone with Urvaśī in the lands of Prayogan and Urvaśī gave birth to several sons who were renowned as Āyu, Amāvasu, Viśvāyu, Śatāyu, Dṛhāyu, and Vanāyu respectively.[24]

The *BrP* only given a detailed description of the career of king Purūravas. Urvaśī is depicted as one of the ladies who became enamoured with the personality of the king and as a result of their union they led a conjugal life which proceeded in an ordinary way. Details of their love-episode and the ups and downs in their life which are found in some Purāṇas are not described here.

URVAŚĪ AND PURŪRAVAS IN THE PADMA PURĀṆA

The legend of Purūravas occurs in the *PdP*[49] where he is described as a monarch of the worlds who could own untold wealth through austerity. He owned the famous seven islands propitiating Lord Brahmā and he could enslave the tyrant Keśī by virtue of his great power and merits. Urvaśī became his consort and remained as his dearest wife.

But it happened, all of a sudden, that Artha, Kāma and Dharma came to him to test his impartial judgement. Purūravas received them with veneration and cordiality and asked them to sit on the seats bedecked with golds, but he showed more attention to Dharma than the other two. At this Artha and Kāma were enraged with him and cursed him saying, "Due to greed you will be mad chasing Urvaśī in the Gandhamādana hill." But Dharma who stood by the king consoled him thus, "You will have a long life, and a pious life, your name will be remembered so long as the sun and moon shine on this planet, but you will have to suffer the pangs of separation from Urvaśī for a long period of sixty years, moving at random. And at the end, you will regain your sweetheart Urvaśī." Thus, saying, they retired to their respective abodes.[50]

Years rolled by and Purūravas, who used to visit Indra's heaven regularly, one day chanced to see Urvaśī along with her mate Citralekhā. They were being kidnapped by the demon Keśī. The king defeated the demon through his power, and sent Urvaśī to Indra. But from that time onward, they were mutually attracted to each other. One day Urvaśī had to play the role of Lakṣmī in a dramatic performance directed by Bharata.[51] Her mates Menakā and Rambhā too began their dancing. Urvaśī donned an appropriate dress and made the required gestures, but at the sight of Purūravas in that place she became wild in passion and missed her dialogue. Then getting enraged with her for disobeying his direction Bharata hurled a curse at Urvaśī to remain for fifty-five thousand years as a creeper on earth. After the end of the curse she would be united with the king.

The story described in the *PdP* may be said to be an imitation of the *MtP*. It also bears similarity with the theme of the *Vikramorvaśīyam*. But one contrast is found: Purūravas of the *PdP* is described as a worshipper of Brahmā whereas the *MtP* says he is the disciple of Janāradana.[52]

URVAŚĪ AND PURŪRAVAS IN THE SKANDA PURĀṆA

The *SkandaP*[54] gives some information with regard to the birth story of Urvaśī. She is said to have been born as a result of the rubbing of the thigh of Nārāyaṇa. The story has affinity with that of the *VāP* and *DvP* respectively, but it lacks the poetic fancy of those in the former Purāṇas (*VāP* and *DvP*). It also lacks the love episode of Purūravas with Urvaśī.

URVAŚĪ AND PURŪRAVAS IN THE AGNI PURĀṆA

The *AgP*[54] states that Purūravas was born of Budha and Ilā. Purūravas married Urvaśī, the celestial *apsarā*, who spent a long period of time in contact with the king. Purūravas is described to have transformed into a *gandharva* and begotten Āyu and other sons in Urvaśī.

URVAŚĪ AND PURŪRAVAS IN THE VARĀHA PURĀṆA

The *VrP*[55] has also given information about the birth of Urvaśī, but this Purāṇa lacks the story of Purūravas. It has mentioned a certain pool which bears association with Urvaśī.[56]

URVAŚĪ AND PURŪRAVAS IN THE KŪRMA PURĀṆA

The *KrP*[57] states that Purūravas married Urvaśī, and she gave birth to Āyu, Amāyu, Vanāyu, Śatāyu, Amtāyu and others but it does not describe stories involving the couple in detail.

URVAŚĪ AND PURŪRAVAS IN THE GARUḌA PURĀṆA

The *GdP*[34] has described the marital life of the couple Purūravas and Urvaśī, from whom six sons were born in course of time.

THE STORY OF VASIṢṬHA AND AGASTYA IN THE MATSYA PURĀṆA

Besides the detailed description of the love episode of Purūravas and Urvaśī, the *MtP*[59] narrates the birth story of Vasiṣṭha and Agastya which is hinted in an early work like the *Ṛgveda* (7, 33, 12) and described in the post-Vedic works. It is said that once Mitra and Varuṇa were absorbed in severe penance in the Badarikāśrama. One day, while the spring season was incarnating itself the Malaya breeze blew, the trees became laden with new sprouts and flowers, and all of a sudden both the gods had a chance to see Urvaśī, busy plucking flowers. She was decked with silk garments and ornaments. They were amazed to see Urvaśī who appeared beautiful possessing eyes like the blue lotuses, and her face shone like the moon. They were deeply captivated and as a result their semen dropped on the skin of the deer but gods' semen does not go in vain. The semen was careful was kept in a pitcher. In course of time, two male children were born out of the semen and later on these two children became renowned as Vasiṣṭha and Agastya.

And the *VișP*[60] states that due to the curse of Nimi, Vasiṣṭha become bodyless and his soul began to wander hither and thither. Luckily at the sight of Urvaśī Mitra-Varuṇa came into a passion and as a result their semen fell on the ground and these were kept in the womb of Urvaśī. Thus, Vasiṣṭha's soul entered their semen. In due course of time Vasiṣṭha regained his earlier form.

URVAŚĪ'S ROLE IN THE CIRCLE OF THE SUN

The *VișP*[61] gives a narrative on the circling of the Sun which takes place every year, with a large number of *yakṣas*, *gandharvas*, serpents, *apsaras*, and *asuras* moving around the Sun. It is stated that in the month of Agrahāyaṇa or Mārgaśīrṣa, Hansa, Kaśyapa, Citrasena, Urvaśī, Takṣa, Mahāpadma move around the Sun. The *DvP*[38] also gives a narrative of similar type. Of course, here the homes of the gods, *apsaras*es and *asuras* are described in a manner that varies from the account in with *VișP*.[63] Therefore, we may assume that the Purāṇas were composed, compiled and edited in different situations and at different times.

URVAŚĪ AND PURŪRAVAS IN THE HARIVAMŚA

The legend of Purūravas and Urvaśī also occurs in the *HmV*,[64] as usual type which bears no significant affinity with the legends described in the Vedas (*ṚV* 10-95) and the post-Vedic works (Purāṇas).[65]

Purūravas and Urvaśī in the Kathā-Sarit-sāgara

The *KSS*[66] of Somadeva is an instance of an artistic work where the author has described the love legend with some innovation. The love story of Purūravas and Urvaśī is in brief as follows.

Purūravas was a devotee of Viṣṇu. And one day he chanced to see Urvaśī in the Nandana Vana of Indra. The moment she beheld him, his sight completely robbed her of her senses. Her condition alarmed the timid minds of Rambhā and her other friends. The king too, when he saw that the nectar of beauty had fainted with thirst that remained unfulfilled, could not bear the burden of sorrow arising from being unable to possess her. Then Viṣṇu who knew all dwellings in the Sea of Milk gave command to Nārada, an excellent hermit, to intervene in this affair so that their union might be effected immediately. Thus, commanded by Viṣṇu Nārada undertook the cause of the lovers and immediately he roused Purūravas from lethargy with his encouraging words. He also promised him extend help to bring about his union with Urvaśī. Then Nārada communicated the order of Viṣṇu to Indra so that this union might be possible. And thus their union took place immediately.

One day Purūravas went to heaven invited by Indra to assist him in a war that was ensuing between him and Mayadharas, the king of *asuras*. In that war the king of the *asuras* was slain, and accordingly Indra held a great feast at which all the nymphs of heaven displayed their skill in dance and music. On that occasion Purūravas was watching Rambhā perform a dramatic dance called '*chalita*' along with her *guru* Tumburu when she suddenly missed her step. The king laughed at this. Then Rambhā said to him sarcastically. "It is a divine dance. I know you are a mortal, then how do you know it."[67] Purūravas answered, "By my association with Urvaśī whatever I know of dance even your teacher Tumburu does not know." When Tumburu heard this he laid his curse on him in his wrath: "Mayest thou be separated from Urvaśī until you propitiate Kṛṣṇa." Purūravas heard the curse and went and told Urvaśī what had happened to him, which was terrible as a 'thunderbolt from the blue'.[68]

Immediately some *gandharvas* swooped down without the king's knowledge and carried Urvaśī to *svargaloka*. When Purūravas came to know of this he realised that the curse of Tumburu was taking effect in this way, and he began his penance for the appeasement of Viṣṇu. The *gandharvas* did not surrender Urvaśī to him. Accordingly the king pleased Viṣṇu with his severe penance, and then Urvaśī was released and her union with the king took place for ever.[69]

The *KSS* shows some novelty, in comparison with the legends described in the Purāṇas when it comes to the love story the couple.

Purūravas is shown a devotee of Viṣṇu. The union of Purūravas and Urvaśī took place through the sympathetic favour of Viṣṇu and in order to get her for ever Purūravas worshipped Viṣṇu in the Badarīkāśrama. Purūravas, experience in the case of practising dance and rhyme flashed a new light in the treaty of music which had been prevailing during his period.[70]

The *Bṛhatkathā* of Guṇādhya also repeats the story in the same manner and diction.

Purūravas and Urvaśī in the Upapurāṇas

Although traditional lore speaks of eighteen Purāṇas (by the side of Mahāpurāṇas) yet the Purāṇa literature extended beyond this traditional number owing to some Upapurāṇas which grew and developed into nebulous form at the hands of compilers in the later period. While some of the Upapurāṇas are extensive and important, a few can rightly claim to have originated much earlier than many of the so-called Mahāpurāṇas now extant.[71] In these Upapurāṇas the epic matter has become entirely subordinate to the ritual element. In continuation of our discussion on the said legend (Purūravas and Urvaśī) we would like to take up the theme as given in some of the Upapurāṇas.

PURŪRAVAS AND URVAŚĪ IN THE KĀLIKĀ PURĀṆA

The *KLP* is one of the Upapurāṇas that contains valuable materials for the study of the social, religious and even political history of Kāmarūpa.[72] It has also dealt with the story of Urvaśī. However, the love episode of Urvaśī and Purūravas is totally omitted from it. Rather she is described to have had an association with Purañjaya, who was none other than Kakustha, and as a result of their union a female child was born, whom she avoided on the eve of her departure. It may be assumed that her nature had borne testimony of a nymph's characteristics. It is also described that she was seduced by some persons Śaṅkara by name, and in another occasion it is described that she was seduced by a Bhairava on the peak of the Himālayas. In a nutshell, this Purāṇa describes Urvaśī as a concubine, who was forced to come into contact with various persons in different situations. Her depiction bears affinity with the state of the *devadāsī* in a later age.

PURŪRAVAS AND URVAŚĪ IN THE VAIṢṆAVA UPAPURĀNAS

Unlike the Purāṇas, the Upapurāṇas related to Viṣṇu also speak of the birth episode of Urvaśī in a colourful style. It is stated that Urvaśī was created by sage Nārāyaṇa who did severe penance in the Badarīkaśrama,[73] where fierce animals like tigers and lions had to remain in non-violence. Apprehending danger from Nārāyaṇa, once Indra sent his *apsarases* along with cupid and the spring season to disturb his penance. But to their utter surprise Nārāyaṇa created a beautiful *apsarā* from his thigh who was Urvaśī. Along with this episode a subordinate story of Nimi and Vasiṣṭha is found described here.

PURŪRAVAS AND URVAŚĪ: VIṢṆUDHARMOTTARA PURĀṆA

It is described in *VDP*[74] that Urvaśī was formed out of the thigh of Nārāyaṇa and Tumburu is said to have cursed Urvaśī for her intense love for Purūravas. And after a long separation, through the intervention of Nārada, Purūravas and Urvaśī were united at Kurukṣetra. The *Viṣṇudharmottara Purāṇa*[74] goes a step further to describe Purūravas as a true devotee of Nārāyaṇa. The king worshipped Him in the *dvādaśī tithi*. And according to the advice of sage Atri, Purūravas performed the *rūpasattra vrata* and consequently attained uncommon physical beauty through the grace of Viṣṇu.

URVAŚĪ: THE MODEL OF ART OF PAINTING

The *VDP* which may be called the source of Indian culture (Section III) is of a very miscellaneous character, treating of grammar, lexicography metrics, and poetics, dancing, singing and music, sculpture and painting (the making of image of gods, and architecture[75] (construction of temples). It is said that Nārāyaṇa invented the art of painting at the very outset. He created Urvaśī after painting her figure on the surface of the earth with a piece of a *sahakara* (mango tree) and taught this art to Viśvakarman.

URVAŚĪ IN THE SAURA PURĀṆA

The *Saura Purāṇa*[76] which belongs to the group of Śaiva Upapurāṇas has also described the story of Urvaśī in a different way. She is found to have and union with Viśvata, son of Vītihotra. We opine that this episode shows slight affinity with the story found in the *Kūrma Purāṇa*.

Urvaśī in the holy places

Not only has Urvaśī occupied a major place in Sanskrit works but it may also be pointed out that just as many holy places in India go after the names of gods and goddesses and sages, so also various pools and places have been associated with her.[77] These are as follows:

URVAŚĪ TĪRTHA

A holy place Vedadvīpa by name is associated with Urvaśī because it is said that in that very place the union between Urvaśī and Purūravas took place. According to this legend the desperate king Purūravas was consoled by Vasiṣṭha who asked him to arrange a sacrifice there. When Purūravas did accordingly Urvaśī visited the place on every *pūrṇimā tithi* and had union with the king. The *Mbh* also speaks of a *tīrtha* which goes after her name.[78]

The *Kālikā Purāṇa* takes the name of Urvaśī with reference to a pool which is named Urvaśī-Kuṇḍa. It has been located near the famous temple Kāmākhyā (Assam) near the Nīlācala mountain. It is to be noted that the ritualistic customs of various idols and pilgrimages are ascribed to this place. And there also lies a stone called Urvaśī Śilā[79] on the bosom of the great Brahmaputra river where many poets of past and present have composed poems in praise of this legendary stone.

Urvaśī in the fairy tales

Urvaśī also appears in the famous fairy tale which goes by the name of *Vikramacarita*[80] or 'Adventures of Vikrama'. Vikrama who was a king on the earth could give expert judgement in connection with dance competitions held at *svargaloka*. The story runs as follows.

A dispute arose between Rambhā and Urvaśī about their dancing talent. Even Indra could not decide the matter peacefully and impartially and at last Nārada informed that Vikramāditya, the ruler of earth, would be able to give suitable judgement in the case. Accordingly, being invited by Indra, Vikramāditya ascended the seat of judgement and on the first day Rambhā exhibited her dance performance, and on the next day Urvaśī exhibited dance according to the *śāstra*s of dancing. Vikramāditya praised Urvaśī for her faultless exhibition in a very eulogistic speech. Indra then questioned the king as to why Urvaśī had been judged the best. The king replied that in dance the first requisite was a perfect dancing body about which the *śāstra*s have enumerated the rules.

> The movement of upper and lower limbs of the body, stepping movements of the waist, head, eyes and ears should be done proportionally with equal balance and attractive resting of the limbs at proper times is necessary. The other important requisites considered by the experts in dancing are mild movements of the chest and good formation of the legs. All of the above movements should be especially practised by the dancer. The main duty of the dancer, before starting even a simple dance, is to move the feet in a balanced rectangular fashion, and both the hands like tender creepers. Moreover the dancer should not show her body in an improper way.
>
> The dancers must have a beautiful moonlike face.

> The arms should be like swinging creepers, shoulders short, the breasts should be full and raised and not be disturbed by the arms and there should be space of the palm of the two hands between the two. The movements of the lips and the thighs should be beautiful, the fingers should be well-shaped.

Urvaśī: Incarnation of Durgā

Urvaśī appears as a lover of the mortal king Purūravas at the very outset but her image has been developed gradually in the later period. As a result she considered as belonging to Durgā, the Ādyaśakti who is located in the Badarīkāśrama, assuming Durgā form in course of time.[80]

Urvaśī also reappears in different[81] works of the later period such as the *Rāmāyṇa Mañjarī* and *Bṛhatkathā*[82] *Mañjarī*, where her birth story and other details are given without the addition of new information.

The *Saundaryalaharī*[83] which belongs to Śaṅkarācārya has described her physical beauty with reference to beauty of Durgā. I would like to quote from it.

> The beauty of your body are like paths of splendour from the fresh sun who brings to mind the sky and the whole wide earth immensed in a red glow from thẹm.
>
> There would be among the heavenly courtesans those whose eyes are as shy as those of timid forest deer and the body of these dancers should be such as to properly express the moods through movements of the limbs while dancing.

We may say that although Urvaśī was a nymph in *svarga-loka*, traditionally she is said to have influenced the world of dance through her excellent training in dance according to the rules laid down in the *Nāṭyaśāstra* and *Nṛtyaśāstra*.

URVAŚĪ AND PURŪRAVAS IN VIKRAMORVARŚĪYAM OF KĀLIDĀSA

Kālidāsa[84], the master poet of India, composed his drama called *Vikramorvaśīyam* on the theme of the legend of Purūravas and Urvaśī. The play consists of five acts, belonging to the class of Troṭaka[85]. It starts with a benediction to Lord Śiva, unlike his other plays. In the prologue the *sūtradhāra* praises merits of the excellent hero (Purūravas) and he hears the screams of the nymphs. Later on it is revealed that the celestial nymph, Urvaśī was forcibly taken away by Keśin, a demon and her companions seek for help to rescue her from the clutches of the demon. Purūravas hurries forward to rescue her from the demon and he returns with the nymph. Thus, the hero and heroine fall in love at first sight, and their union lasts for a while. Thereafter, Citraratha descends from the air and reports as to how his friend Urvaśī had been forcibly taken away by Keśin. He congratulates the king for rescuing Urvaśī from the demon and adds that along with her two friends (nymphs), Urvaśī is to come to heaven with him in no time. Then Urvaśī starts for heaven, hesitatingly looking behind on the pretext of her necklace getting entangled in the thickets of creepers[86] and the king also departs with a heavy heart saying:

> This nymph of heaven is off with my heart forcibly out of my body as through the mid-regions of her sire she flies. So flies the swan with a fibre from the lotus stalk the end of which is broken.

The Second Act opens with a conversation between the *vidūṣaka* and the maid servant of the queen before whom the *vidūṣaka* discloses the love-lorn condition of the king, who is pining for a celestial nymph. Nipunikā learns the secret of the cat which has been let out of the bag and hurries to inform the queen. The king enters in a state of absent-mindedness, with the sights and sounds of the Pramadavana no longer able to remove his mental agony cherished for Urvaśī. The *vidūṣaka* repeatedly tries his best to comfort him with words. Just then Urvaśī along with Citralekhā moving in the air reaches the place and hear about his intense for her. She drops a letter[87] written on a birch bark breathing her love. The king reads it and gives it to the *vidūṣaka* for safekeeping. They are now sure that the king is nose deep in love. At that moment Citralekhā appears with Urvaśī. They exchange a few words, but their conversation is cut short by the arrival of the Devadūta who informs them that they should return to heaven for joining in a dramatic performance to be directed by Bharata.[88] Their union ends abruptly. Urvaśī departs, the king wants to take consolation by reading the letter she wrote. But the *vidūṣaka* replies with despair that it is lost somewhere. The king, out of remorse, takes the *vidūṣaka* to task for his carelessness. In the meantime Ausinari, the queen, enters the grove, discovers the letter of Urvaśī and comes to know of Urvaśī's love for Purūravas. She refuses to appear before the king, who attempts to sooth her.

The Third Act begins with a conversation between the two pupils of the sage Bharata, which reveals that Urvaśī had cut a sorry figure in the dramatic performance by disobeying Bharata's direction: she uttered the name of Purūravas in place of Puruṣottama out of carelessness, as her mind was preoccupied with the thought of Purūravas. Bharata had cursed her, but Indra intervenes with the words that she would leave heaven to dwell on earth with her lover Purūravas until she sees the face of her offspring.

Now the king enters the terrace of the crystal pavilion along with the *vidūṣaka*. Here Urvaśī and her mate remain concealed by virtue of their divine power, and they overhear the conversation of the two. Urvaśī is delighted at the decision of the queen, that she would reconcile herself to her lot. Urvaśī gets down and covers the king's eyes. The king joys know no bounds. Citralekhā departs for heaven requesting the king's to take care of her friend Urvaśī.

The Fourth Act begins with a dialogue between the dejected mind of Citralekhā and Sahajanyā informing that Urvaśī had entered the Kumāravana and Kumara, being enraged at the king for his look at Udayavatī, a *vidyādharī*, had cursed Urvaśī and she had been transformed into a creeper. Purūravas becomes wild at the sudden loss of Urvaśī, and goes on enquiring about her whereabouts. After long enquiry he discovers a magic stone in the grove, and hears a voice asking him to pick it up. He embraces the creeper that immediately gets transformed to Urvaśī. He is overjoyed to find his beloved after a prolonged absence and suffering, and they return to his capital in great joy.

The Fifth Act starts with the *vidūṣaka* informing that the loving couple have celebrated the moon festival at the capital. In the meanwhile a noise is heard for the magic-stone has been stolen by a vulture which, however, falls pierced by the arrow of a youthful archer. The arrow bears the name of Āyu, son of Urvaśī and Purūravas. The king is now full of confusion as regards Āyu's identity as his own son, which appears to be a miracle to him. In the meantime a woman arrives there from a hermitage with a gallant boy, the younger archer, who is educated in the duties of the warrior caste. Since he had violated the rule of the hermitage, he had to return to his mother. Urvaśī arrives and admits her parentage, but after a while she starts -, remembering the condition set by Indra previously on the eve of her journey to earth — that she should be back at the sight of her child.

The king, with a heavy sigh, says, "How hostile to man's happiness is fate." He determines to retire to the forest, offering the responsibility of the kingdom to his son Āyu, as he would be unable to bear the pangs of separation from Urvaśī. Suddenly, Nārada appears amidst them with the happy news sent by Indra, the chief of the gods, that says:

> You are a worthy ally in the wars. Therefore do not relinquish your arms and this Urvaśī shall be your wife as long as you live.

Now Urvaśī feels that "a barbed arrow has been extracted from her bosom". In the meantime Rambhā descends from the air bringing materials for the coronation ceremony of Āyu, the son of the couple. Āyu is coronated in the due manner and all are happy in the long run.

DEVIATION AND INNOVATION BROUGHT ABOUT BY KĀLIDĀSA

In introducing the theme in the form of a play Kālidāsa has effected many changes in the theme wherever necessary. The following innovations were made by the poet while treating the theme in the play.

1. The conditions put forth by Urvaśī, which are mentioned in the *Brāhmaṇa*s (ŚPB), have not included in the play. Kālidāsa has made an innovation in the form of a condition that the lovers would have to part from each other if Urvaśī was to see the face of the son born of their union.
2. The *gandharva*s' trick to cause their separation was felt by Kālidāsa as uncalled for. Therefore, it has been dropped from the play.
3. The lambs which Urvaśī kept beside her couch, and which the *gandharva*s stole according to the ancient version of the legend, are not mentioned in the drama.
4. Urvaśī separates from the hero at the end of the Vedic legend, and, thus, the Vedic story was tragic. It has been transformed into a story with a happy ending by the dramatist.
5. Kālidāsa has introduced new personalities and ideas

to make the theme suitable for the purpose of a drama.

I. Auśinarī is brought into the drama as the queen, who is the rival of the heroine.

II. *Vidūṣaka* is the stereotyped companion of the king (hero), as is usually found in Sanskrit drama.

III. The companions of Urvaśī namely, Sahajanyā and Citralekhā, are depicted as raising an alarm at the rape of Urvaśī by Kaśin and, thus, the dramatist skilfully draws the king's attention towards Urvaśī and the lovers are brought together for the first time.

IV. The curse motive which is usual in Sanskrit drama is introduced. The curse is hurled by sage Bharata to throw away Urvaśī from the Court of Indra for a stipulated period of time and she is united with the mortal king, Purūravas. In this way Kālidāsa has dropped the curse of Mitra and Varuṇa, and instead introduced Bharata's curse.

V. Another curse of Kumāra is introduced in the theme, of course newly, to separate Urvaśī from Purūravas for sometime. This happens when the heroine unhesitatingly enters the Kumāravana.

VI. The birth of Āyu and his concealment by Urvaśī is a major innovation made by Kālidāsa. In this drama Āyu is very carefully introduced towards the end of the drama to effect separation of the lovers, but the situation is saved by the introduction of another novelty by the poet, namely, Nārada's proclamation of Indra's verdict that the lovers would remain in permanent union. Lastly Rambhā is introduced as a new character to bring the materials of coronation for the youthful Āyu to be consecrated as a *yuvarāja*.

Thus, Kālidāsa has transformed an insipid story into a tasteful one full of lucid sentiment and has turned the tragedy into a comedy.

Last but not least the dramatist, very imaginatively, has introduced as many dramatic personages as required for a dramatic performance.

References

1. *Rām*, 7, 56, 9-28.
2. *Ibid.*, 7, 55, 1-20.
3. *Ibid.*, 7, 56, 4-10.
4. *Ibid.*, 7, 56, 13-21.
5. Read 7, 56, 22-5 Urvaśī IV.
6. *Rām*, 7, 57-5.
7. Vide Ch. 2, Section I.
8. For details, see Sarmah, T., *Vaidik Kālina Pravāha*, pp. 96. Dandekar, R.N., 'The two births of Vasiṣṭha', *H. Guntert Comm. Volume*, 425-32, *Vedic Mythological Tract*, Delhi, 1979, pp. 332-50.
9. *Mbh*. 1. 44, 10, 74-68, 75, 18-25;
   2. 10-11;
   3. 46-1-3-29, 3, 46-44-58;
   4. 2-4-13, 7-9;
   5. 110-35;
   6. 117-14;
   7. 60-6;
   8. 29-66;
   9. 332-21-25;
   10. 165, 14-40
10. Read *Mbh*. 1, 123-64-5:

    menakā, shajanyā, ca karṇikā, puñjikasthalā ||
    ṛtusthalā ghṛtācī ca, viśvācī, pūrvacittiyāpī |
    umlocitica vikhyāta pramlocali ca ita daśa |
    urvaśyekādasī tacamagagascayātalocanā ||
11. Read. 1, 75-18-24:

    purūravastata vidyanilaya . . . .
    sa hi gandharvalokastannvasya sahita virat ||

12. Read *Mbh*, 3, 110-35-7:

tasya retaḥ praṣanṣkanda dṛṣṭvāpsarammvaśim
apsupaspra tu rājonmṛga taccapivattadā ।।

sahathyana tṛṣitā sa garbhinyashavanṛpa
amaghatvadvidh ścaiva bhabitaddaiva nimittvād ।।

tasyam mṛgyam sambhustusya putramahanrsih ṛṣyaśṛṅga ।।

12. Read *Mbh*. 2, 10-10-12:

miśrakeśī ca rambhā ca citrasenā susmitā cārunetrā
ghṛtācī ca menakā puñjikasthalā viśvācī ।।

sahajanyā ca pūrvacitti, urvaśī irā vargā ca
sauraveyī ca samici vudvabudalatā etā ।।

sahasrcānya nṛtyagītaviśāradā upatiṣṭhanti
dhandam gondharva psarasam gataḥ ।।

13. Read *Mbh*. 7-24:

tathaivāpsarassa rajana gandharvas ca manaramāḥ ।
nṛtya vāditatra gitamcā hasya sca bibidhāirāpi
ramayanti sma nroate devarajani śata kratum ।।

14. Vide, 3, 43-29-30:

ghṛtācī menakā rambhā pūrvacittiḥ svayamprabhā ।
urvaśī miśrakeśī ca daṇḍagaurī varuthinī ।

gopālī sahajanyā ca kambhajonī prajagārā ।
citrasenā citralekhā svāhā ca madhurasvarā ।।

etascanya sca nanrta sṭaṭhā tatra schasrasaḥ ।।

15. Read *Mbh*. 3, 45-1-21-26:

pārthasya cakṣaravasya saktam bijnaya vasavaḥ ।
gandharvaraja jacachadya prahita psarasam varam ।

urvaśī parasabyaghra sapatisthata phālājanam ।।
sacacha tvam hi yathakama najamisyanyaham sakham ।।

Vide 3, 46-1-2:

urvaśī cakaratsnanam pārthadarśanlālasā ।

atibidhenamanas manmathena pradipitā ।।

16. 3, 46-20-2:

abhivādaye tvām pravaripsanasam vare
himanjnapayase devi presya steha mupa sthitaḥ ।।

17. 3, 46-29-32:

tavapitrabhyanajnata gatahi svam svam gṛham suraḥ ।
priyami kura mahendrasya nāma caibatmana sca ha ।।

18. *Ibid*., 3, 46-40-41:

guru guru tara me tvam māma tvam vañśabardhini । ।

19. *Ibid.*, 3, 46-43-44:

jāt prasida na mamarta bisarjiyatymakarsi ।
icchayena ca santapam bhaktyam ca bhaga manada । ।

20. *Ibid.*, 3, 46-49-1:

yasman man nabhinandethah kamabana basani gatam ।
jasmattam nartanaḥ pārtha stremadheymanava varjitaḥ
apumaniti bikhyata saṇḍavardhicarisyasi । ।

21. *Ibid.*, 3, 46-57-9:

ajnatabasa bastabya vabadhbhi bhutalinajha ।
varsamenam bihatyeva tataḥ pumstamabapsyasi । ।

Read. Mani Vettam, *Purunica Encyclopaedia*, Motilal Banarsidass, Delhi 19, C.U., p. 813.

Vide 12-332-(149)-19-25:

pancadueta prabhitaya bhrasamutphullalocana ।
urvaśīya bacanam sratva sunaḥ paramadharabit
kṛtāñjali pataḥ sarvaḥ niriksantye smadevataḥ

22. Read *Hv*. 26-1-49:

budheśya to mahārāja vidvanputra purarevaḥ
vejesvi danasitam sca yajva bipula dakṣiṇaḥ
rajyam sa karayamasa prajaje pṛthivipatiha
uttara jhanavitira pralisthane mehayasaḥ । ।

23. Read Macdonell, A.A., *History of Sanskrit Literature*, 1899, p. 247.

Vide Winternitz, M., *A History of Indian Literature*, p. 389.

"The Indians however regard also the *Harivaṁśa:* A work which is in reality a Purāṇa and is also occasionally called *Harivaṁśa Purāṇa* as part of the *Mahāhārata.*"

24. *Hmv*, 26:

brahmaśāpabhibhatva samānuṣam samapadyata
a laim to sa varabaha samayamupa sthita

. . . . . .

gṛhtāmātra tatāhāra kālemekam pārthitaḥ

25. Read Macdonell, A.A., *History of Sanskrit Literature*, 1899, p. 320.

KSS 3, 3-4-30:

āsit purūravasa nāma rājā paramaviṣṇavaḥ
abhudbhaviva nakepi yasya pratinata gatiḥ
bhramontam nandane jāta tan dadarśa kilapsarā

26. *KSS*, 3.3, 19-21; 3.3.4, 27-30:

purūravasa tapasa tenaccyatamatasy

tatprasādena gandharva mumucustasy cavarśim । ।

sapantalabdhaya yuktaḥ punapyasarasa toga ।
divyasisa raja bubhāge bhaganbhutalabatyapi ।

27. *KSS* 33, 22-24:

28. See, Shri Hirendralal, B.B., *Kathā-sarit-sāgara*, tr., Calcutta, 1975.

29. Read Hirendralal, B.B., *Kathā-sarit-sāgara*, Calcutta, 1975, p. 11.

30. Aiyer C. Ramaswami, *The Cultural Heritage of India*, vol. 2, Calcutta, 1962, p. 271.

    Also Read Macdonell, A.A., *A History of Sanskrit Literature*, Varanasi, Patna, 1899, p. 254.

31. Read *KLP* 49, 59-70, 89-17-22:

    akadā to kākatṣthaḥ himavantam mahagirini ।
    mṛgayayā jagannatha mṛgaccapinipatita । ।

    lamvantim suralakat to bhariprati todurvaścim ।
    visnaya pabistatsta sanonvesyam dadarśa ha । ।

    urvaśī ramayamasa girikanje yathaspa
    athaikada bhairavasan urvaśīnamapsarvarsam suganadhipat

32. Read *Studies in the Upapurāṇas* Vol. (ch. 102-3) Sanskrit College, Calcutta, R.C. Hazra, Gauhati University K.K. Handiqui Library, Guwahati 14, Kamrup, Assam.

33. *Ibid.*, *The Major Vaiṣṇava Upapurāṇas*, Ch. 124.

34. *Ibid.*, 35-43, Vol. II *Viṣṇudharmottara Upapurāṇa*, p. 181.

    Read Aiyar C.P. Ramaswamy, *The Cultural Heritage of India*, p. 278.

35. Read *Saura Purāṇa*, Chakravati Sri Subodh Kumar — Translation from Sanskrit into Bengali version, pp. 65-7, Visrata Urvaśī-Saṁvād, A. Mukharjee and Co. Pvt. Ltd., 2 Bankim Chatterjee Street, Calcutta.

36. Read *Immortal India*, vol. I, J.H. Dave, p. 202, General Editors, K.M. Munshi, R.R. Divakar, Bharatiya Vidya Bhavan, Chanpatty, Bombay, 1970.

37. Some of the most important *tīrtha*s of Assam were Siddheśvarī, Apūrṇabhava, Urvaśī, Manikarṇeśvar, Pāṇḍanātha, Kāmākhyā, Aśvakrasta, Hayagrīva, etc.

    Read also *Mbh*, 3, 54-136:

    urvaśītīrthamāsādya tataḥ samasramam budhaḥ
    kambhakarmāśrame snātvā pūjyate bhubimonareḥ

    Read also *Brahma Purāṇa* 170.1-23:

    urvaśītīrthamakhyātamasvamedhabhalapradaya ।

snadradana mahādeva vasadeva reangdirghi ||

Vide Mani Vettam *'Pauranica'*, p. 60, Motilal Banarsidass, 1975.

38. Read the note no. 18, p. 202. The place may be now located near Umānanda, close to D.C. Court. Guwahati.

Also read *Mbh*, 3.89-157, 13-25-46

Ibid., *Mbh.*, 7.60 Droṇaparva.

39. Read Banerjee, P., *Apsaras in Indian Dance*, pp. 103-4.

Dvātruṣa Puttalika, 7-12:

vikramana bhanitam deva urtyeprathamamanda sauskrva pradhānam taya cuktam nṛtyasaste ||

anucyaniyam caratanmaganam calapadata mati kustisrva kst karnanam samarapata ||

tatamarandranon vikramakam vastadena sammubya dadau

Read also *Mālavikāgnimitram*, Kālidāsa.

40. Read Vettam Mani 'Paurānica', p. 160, Motilal Banarsidass, Delhi, Patna, Varanasi, 1974.

41. Read Macdonell, A.A., *A History of Sanskrit Literature*, p. 319.

"It is entitled *Bṛhatkathā Mañjarī* and is only about one-third as long as the *Kathā-sarit-sāgara*."

Also read *Rāmāyaṇa Mañjarī*

atrāntare sudhāsindhu mitrāvaruṇasaṅgata |
purū dadarsata kantamurvasamscayagatam ||

42. Read *Bṛhatkathā Mañjarī*, 6, 114-23:

purapurūravase nāme raja, bhabhuvabhami ondarpa ||

43. Read S.L. Sankaracarya, ed. by W. Norman Broon, University of Peninsula, Cambridge Harvard University, 1958.

jannccayamiste tarawatarani srisaraniti |
divamsarvaurvim sranani maghamsmarati yaḥ ||

bhavantayasya trasyadavanaharina salinanayanaḥ
saharvasya nasyaḥ kati kati na gravarna gonikaḥ ||

SL 31-1-2

alaḥ pururasasidraja paramadharmika
urvaśyam janayanasa sat patrasprathita gasaḥ ||

44. Read Keith, A.B., *The Sanskrit Drama*, p. 149.

45. (a) Macdonell, A.A., *A History of Sanskrit Literature*, p. 303.

(b) *Sāhitya Darpaṇa (SD)*: *saptasta nava pañcakam divyamānuṣa sansrayam traṭakanāma tat prāhaḥ pratya kam savidūṣakam*, 6th *pariccheda*

(c) Keith, A.B., *Sanskrit Drama*, p. 351.

(d) A Troṭaka is a type of Rūpaka where the Viduṣaka appears only in Acts II, III and V, p. xxvi,

Devadhar, C.R., ed., *Works of Kālidāsa, Kālidāsa, His Date and Works*, Introduction.

46. Read *PdmP*, p. 12, 12-52.

47. *MtP*, p. 24, 10, 32.

48. *Ibid.*, Act 2 *jatprastava munitana bhurja patrae vikramorvaśīyam sampadituttariam bhabitumicsami* ।

49. (a) Read — *Bharat Vākyam*

(b) See Bharata *Nāṭyaśāstra*

(c) Apte, Vaman Shivaram, *The Students' Sanskrit-English Dictionary*.

(d) Bharata, son of Duṣyanta and Śakuntalā, who becomes a universal monarch (*cakravartin*), India being called Bhāratavarṣa after him. He was a remote ancestor of the Kauravas and Pāṇḍavas.

(e) Brother of Rāma, Son of Kaikeyī and Daśaratha.

(f) An Ancient Sage, who is supposed to have been the founder of the science of music and dramaturgy.

(i) An actor, a stage player

(ii) A hired soldier or mercenary

(iii) A barbarian — mountaineer

(iv) An epithet of Agni

samāptajapyam vratinam svasataiḥ pavibaritam anadhyaye kadācita bharatam naṭyakavidam, *BN* 1, 2.

Sāhityadarpaṇa (SD): *saptastanavapañcakam divyamanuṣasan-srayam/troṭkanama tat prah pratyankam savidusakam*/6th Paricceda, 273, 282.

A *troṭaka* is a type of *rūpaka* where the *vidūṣaka* appears (in *Vik*. in Acts II, III and V, *vidūṣaka* figures).

50. *Vik.*, 1, 13.

51. *Ibid.*, 1, 16.

52. *Ibid.*, 1, 18: *asa mano me prasabham sarirat*
pituḥ padam madhyamamutpatanti ।
surmgana karsatikhanditgrat
sūtram mrnaladiva rajahamso ।।

53. *Ibid.*, 2, 17.

54. *Ibid.*, 5, 9.
55. *Ibid.*, 5, 9.
56. *Ibid.*, *ammahe salyamiva hṛdayad apanitam* ।
ahu śdyaṃ me hṛdayādpasitasiva.

5

Legend of Urvaśī and Purūravas in Modern Literature

Urvaśī Jananī

THE *Urvaśī Jananī*[1] (Urvaśī Mother) is a unique novel composed by Dipak Chandra[2] in Bengālī language where the legend of Purūravas and Urvaśī is depicted with a modern outlook, with new diction and treatment. The story is described briefly thus:

Urvaśī was born of Nārāyaṇa,[3] who was absorbed deeply in meditation, when he chanced to have a union with an *apsarā*, sent by Indra, who apprehended danger of losing his supremacy in heaven. As a result of their union a female child was born who became renowned as Urvaśī in due course. But the female child was abandoned by Nārāyaṇa and the *apsarā*. She shared common characteristics with other *apsaras*es like Menakā.[4] Luckily a merchant Dhanakubera by name who was also issueless discovered her and he brought her up with care and tender affection. The child grew up into a bewitching beauty. Many suitors sought her hand to marry and even Indra sent a messenger to Dhanakubera with the proposal that such a type of delicate lady should enhace the beauty of *svargaloka*, the eternal place of joy and merriment. At this her foster parents were in a dilemma and were not in a position to repudiate the proposal sent by Indra. Urvaśī came to know about the situation and sent her parents and she cursed her bewitching beauty. While pondering over her fate in this way she was caught hold of by a lustful demon Keśin[5] all of a sudden just like a wolf dog catches a stag in the forest. She found herself in a helpless condition and cried aloud for help. In the meanwhile, Prurūravas, who had finished his meditation, heard the screams of a woman and hurriedly went there to extend his help. He defeated the abductor after a fierce battle and rescued Urvaśī and took her to his harem. Thus, by the grace of god and fortune she got rid of the lustful eyes of Indra and engrossed herself in deep love with the king. She attained mortal love of the king and soon realised that she was stepping into motherhood. She bore a child in due course of time. But their happy days were actually short-lived. As Indra had been repudiated, he was enraged. He sent a troop of armies under the leadership of Viśvāvasu,[6] the *gandharva* chief, to encamp at Kumāravana. This unpleasant news incited Purūravas. And he came to know that owing to his unmindfulness of the royal duty of providing security of the empire, Indra was causing fear in his mind. Purūravas was at a loss what to do in this critical juncture. He realised that Urvaśī was the root of all misfortune and adversity. He made up his mind to abandon Urvaśī to get rid of unnecessary battle and bloodshed.

Urvaśī came to know of the intention of the king, but at the same time she began also cherishing in her heart an eagerness for Indra. So with a view to having an interview with the chief of the gods she proceeded secretly to the Kumāravana in the guise of a young prince. Indra was astonished to see her attractive countenance and personality. Urvaśī could no longer conceal her actual identity, disclosed herself before Indra, and as a result they had their union in the remote camp at Kumāravana.

Purūravas also desired that Urvaśī should belong to Indra, because he valued his empire Pratiṣṭhānapura more than Urvaśī.[7] In the meantime Urvaśī gave birth to a son named Āyuraji.[8] Her motherly heart pined for the offspring.

She exclaimed, "Marriage means a bondage, it is a kind of tie of selfishness".[9]

Urvaśī proceeded towards heaven, met Indra, who accepted her gladly, and, thus, she spent a long period of time in association with Indra and came to learn of the licentious nature of Indra. And far more, Indra being well-versed in diplomacy planned to bring an end to a political rivalry with Mitra and Varuṇa[10] through Urvaśī. They also had cherished a weakness for Urvaśī from the very beginning. He advised Urvaśī to meet Mitra-Varuṇa so that he might be able to kill two birds with one stone. Therefore, Indra arranged a musical performance where Uravśī would take the leading role. This was arranged only for bringing an end to the burning rivalry within the royal family. He invited Viśvasvasu, the lord of *gandharvas*, Purūravas, the former husband of Urvaśī, and many other respectable guests to attend. At the end of the musical function Urvaśī had an interview with Purūravas, when they liesurely exchanged their thoughts after a long interval. The king departed with a heavy heart.

Urvaśī happened to meet Arjuna, the middlemost brother of the Pāṇḍavas, who visited Indraloka at the advice of his brothers to undergo a course of training in celestial weapons, which would be helpful in future as and when there might be a war with the Kauravas. He learnt thoroughly the art of archery and mastered the art of war under the guidance of Kārttikeya, the commander-in-chief of the gods, in broad daylight and at the same time learnt the art of dance and music under the guidance of Urvaśī at night. But Indra had his own suspicion regarding Arjuna's visit to *svargaloka*, because he apprehended that Kṛṣṇa might have sent him with the intention of invading *svargaloka*.[11]

However, Arjuna had a chance to spend a period of three long years at *svargaloka* but the excessive lust and passion of Urvaśī which she expressed before Arjuna made him rather careful and ultimately sterner than before. Arjuna politely refused her appeal and in return showed reverence to her like his mother Kuntī.[12] Being rejected she departed to her apartment with a heavy heart.

Now Urvaśī could realise thoroughly that although Indra loved her and kept her at *svargaloka* he never desired to give her the honour of motherhood but rather placed her in the rank of courtesans.[13] She once again could realise her mistake and she recollected the tender face of her child Āyu who had been left at the harem of Purūravas under the care of a nurse. The motherly instinct had pierced her heart and mind through and through. She was uptil now deprived of motherly affection. But now, she desired to hear the sweet sound of her son calling her *mā mā*, 'my mother'. The eternal blessing of the world in the form of a son made her wild at heart. Her heart finally is seen running towards Pratiṣṭhānapura where her husband Purūravas and affectionate son Āyu resided and were waiting with all eagerness for the arrival of Urvaśī.[14]

The work, *Urvaśī Jananī* is found to have deviated from the original sources on many points which may be enumerated below.

The *Urvaśī Jananī* is a novel work which may be categorised in the rank of 'epic' novel. The writer, Dipak Chandra has reconstructed a good number of novels based on the two epics, i.e., the *Rām* and *Mbh*, with new style and treatment like Ram Kumar Varma in Hindī literature.[15]

Dipak Chandra has deviated from the *Ṛgvediç* (X.95) and Brāhmaṇic (*ŚPB*) sources, and instead he has added that Urvaśī was born of Nārāyaṇa, from which the *DvP* and *VāP* also differ to some extent. Urvaśī was left alone and she was brought up by a merchant just as Śakuntalā was brought up by Kaṇva, the venerable sage. But the episode of Urvaśī cannot be ranked with Śakuntalā of Kālidāsa at all. The suitors' wedding proposal for Urvaśī is a novel creation as is also Indra's proposal.

The rescual of Urvaśī from the clutches of Keśīn as described here has similarity with the episode in post-Vedic literature. But their subsequent union after the fierce battle is not mentioned in that literature though it has slight similarity with what is given in the *Vikramorvaśiyam* of Kālidāsa. The novelist has deviated from the original sources and added substantially new ideas with his imagination in order to enhance the curiosity in the minds of the readers. The encampment of Viśvāvasu at Kumāravana by the order of Indra is also an innovation of the writer. Indra's conspiracy to attack Purūravas and Purūravas' attempt to forsake Urvaśī in fear of Viśvāvasu are new elements added to the bulk, deviating from the original source. Urvaśī approaching Indra and her surrender to Indra has lowered her position. The interview with Indra in the Kumāravana has no poetic and moral charm at all. Arjuna's retaliation of her follows the legend depicted in the *Mahābhārata*. It lacks gravity, and Indra's apprehension regarding the reasons for Arjuna's training in archery and his learning of dance in the heaven, bear no great value. But the realisation of Urvaśī that Indra wanted to keep her as a courtesan for ever and did not intend to upgrade her position to the rank of a mother, the highest status of a lady, draws universal appeal towards Urvaśī. This leads her to return to the capital of the king Purūravas. The twist in the story projects Urvaśī in a new light as one who wants to be a mother like many other women in the world.

Urvaśī: Rāmdhārī Singh Dinakar

In the modern age, Rāmdhārī Singh Dinakar[16] has composed a fine *kāvya* entitled *Urvaśī*[17] based on the old legend of Urvaśī and Purūravas. Below we have given a summary of the story of his work and the innovations he carried out upon the original theme. The form of the work is that of an epic.

The *Urvaśī* of Dinakar consists of five cantos. It starts with a conversation between the *sūtradhāra* and *naṭī*. They note that in the calm atmosphere, they can hear the sounds of anklets, which indicate the advent of the heavenly nymphs who are none other than Menakā and Rambhā. Rambhā is first shown advocating the superiority of heaven. Menakā, however, retorts that being a divine being she longs for mortal happiness which seems to be superior to that of heaven. Rambhā looks down upon such mortal happiness. Sahajanyā, one of her friends, makes enquires about the longing for mortal love by saying to Menakā "Your mind longs for someone of the earth like Urvaśī's. Perhaps some handsome person has captivated your heart."[17]

Rambhā asks Sahajanyā why Urvaśī has not joined their company. Then Sahajanyā mentions the abduction of Urvaśī by a demon Keśin who swooped over Urvaśī while she was returning from the castle of Kubera, and informs that luckily she was rescued by Purūravas who happened to hear her screams and finally defeated the demon after a duel with him. In the meantime by mere exchange of glances Purūravas and Urvaśī had fallen in love with each other.[18] Sahajanyā gives information on the love episode before the rest of the *apsaras*es in the absence of Urvaśī.

But Rambhā speaks ill of Urvaśī's love towards the king. She says, "We, the *apsaras*es, are not created to remain with anyone on a permanent basis. We are born to please gods and mortals for a while. We never seek to remain embraced in the arms of someone for ever,[19]" and she adds that they cannot let themselves lose all the beauty of their delicate and divine charms. The *apsaras*es should leave the outer part like a snake. But Menakā replies by taking the side of mortals. Then Citralekhā retorts saying that Urvaśī gets wild in the absence of Purūravas and is tormented out of passion. Urvaśī often goes down on the earth to meet Purūravas. The king is also enamoured of Urvaśī and has forgotten his former wife because Urvaśī pre-occupies his thoughts. But Auśinarī, the first wife of the king, having seen the pensive mood and bewildering movement of her lord, suspected that the king was coming into contact with some unknown lady. So in order to have his love, she had started worshipping the Moon god.

The second chapter begins with the conversation between the queen and a lady mate called Nipuṇikā through whom the queen comes to know that her husband is in deep love with Urvaśī. Although the queen is affirmed in her suspicion by learning everything about her husband's motive, yet as a case, she does not die out of jealousy. She comes to know that her husband has started for the Gandhamādana mountain with a view to arranging a sacrifice desiring a son (up to this time Purūravas and remained without any offspring). Therefore, the vow of chastity of a wife is essential for this purpose.

Nipuṇikā and Madanikā are talking about the nature of the male persons, who are supposed to be the prey of beautiful and lustful ladies like Urvaśī. Even lion-like indomitable persons have to fall at the feet of the ladies of exquisite beauty. In the meanwhile Kañcukī arrives with the news that the king is observing the *puterṣṭi* sacrifice upon the hill, but on the other hand, the queen is bemoaning of her absence and has argued that they cannot have offspring. She says that where her husband stays that place is equal to paradise and there the flowers would remain in bloom.[20]

The third chapter is the description of the love sport of the couple. This is a long narrative in the *kāvya*.[21]

The fourth chapter is an innovation of the poet's fancy and skill and is rich in imagination. Āyu, son of the loving couple, has been brought up by the sage Cyavana and Sukanyā in their hermitage. Urvaśī and Purūravas are deprived of their son due to the curse hurled by Bharata.[22] The incident occurred in this way. One day while Urvaśī was absorbed deeply in thought of the king, Bharata arrived all of a sudden and asked for alms. But as she was absorbed in deep thought she could not respond to his presence. Therefore, being enraged, Bharata cursed her severely that they would remain on earth as long as they did not have a look at their son's face; after which, Urvaśī would have to depart from her husband. Therefore, they were not told about the birth of the child by Cyavana. Here the episode of Cyavana and Sukanyā is intermingled in a new style.[23]

The fifth chapter starts with the news that Urvaśī is proceeding towards Purūravas and they pass sixteen years in harmony. One night the king has a terrible dream. The next day he calls the ministers and astrologers to his Court and informs them of the dream. In the dream he saw an elephant loitering to and fro in the forest where he visited the hermitage of sage Cyavana, and chanced to see a boy, whose physical appearance and personality attracted him very much and while he had attempted to embrace the boy, the latter had vanished immediately. He moved to get up and discovered that Urvaśī was sleeping beside him. All these happenings had appeared like a picture drawn on a canvas. The astrologers hear everything and foretell him that he should retire to the forest and his son should be crowned in his place. But the king is sure that up to that time he has not possessed any child, and he considers it to be impossible.

In the meanwhile Sukanyā arrives along with Āyu and narrates the past events. The curse begins to take effect and Urvaśī immediately ascends to heaven. The king having seen her departure gets wild and tries to march against the gods. But he hears a divine voice with consoling words that he should enthrone his son in his place. Auśinarī comes to learn that the king has determined to proceed towards the forest. But she makes up her mind to stay in the kingdom with Āyu.[24]

DEVIATIONS FROM OTHER WORKS ON THE THEME

1. The story of the epic is treated here with novelty. The poet has shown his imaginative skill here, and such imaginative narration is lacking in the Ṛgvedic legend (95).

2. Unlike the *Vikramorvaśīyam* of Kālidāsa the love affair begins at the time of the abduction of Urvaśī by Keśin which occurs in several works of post-Vedic literature (*MtP*, for instance). They have fallen in love with each other at the first sight. Of course, this episode is described through the conversation of her two mates.[25]

3. The conversation that takes place between Menakā and Rambhā is not found in the original legend (*ṚV*, 10, 95 and *ŚPB*, and also in the Purāṇas). Menakā hankers after mortal love which Rambhā rejects, and this is a new style of treatment of the legend.

4. Here too, as in the *Vikramorvaśīyam* of Kālidāsa, the mind of Auśinarī, the chief queen, is suspicious regarding the absent mindedness and love-lorn condition of her husband Purūravas. But she is portrayed as an ideal chaste lady of traditional Hindu family. Unlike other women (such as Śakuntalā) she is described as having no children. Hence she has never attempted to stand in the way of her husband, who may expect a child or in contact with Urvaśī offspring to keep the continuity of the family for generations to come.[26]

5. The events leading to the curse hurled by Bharata on Urvaśī mentioned here are not found in the *Vikramorvaśīyam* of Kālidāsa; in the latter, the events are narrated differently. They are also not described in such manner in the Ṛgvedic legend and in some Purāṇas. (*MtP*, for instance). But the episode of the

curse of Bharata in the epic of Rāmdhārī Singh Dinkar bears resemblance with that of the curse of Durvāsā in the *Śakuntalā* of Kālidāsa.[27]

6. In the *Vikramorvaśīyam* Indra intervenes to mitigate the effect of the curse to bring about a union of the king and Urvaśī.[28] But in the said (Hindī) epic such a role of Indra has not been shown.

6. The dream dreamt by the king is dealt with novelty the style and diction of the poet contribute much to this. The description of the dream is a marvellous one. The prediction of the astrologer and the divine voice with its consoling words are similar to descriptions found in epics like *Buddhacarita* and *Raghuvaṁśa*.[29] It bears the ideas of Hindu life, and the doctrine of the Hindu scriptures.

7. Āyu, the son of Purūravas and Urvaśī, was crowned in the epic and the king is seen to have retired to the forest but in the *Vikramorvaśīyam* the loving couple, in spite of knowing about their son and seeing him have a chance to remain on earth by the grace of Indra. This has bridged the gulf between the heaven and earth.[30] It may be said here that Purūravas is the symbol of *puruṣa*: he is the symbol of *sanātana puruṣa* (*dharma*) and Urvaśī is the symbol of *sanātanī nārī* in the world.[31] The role of Menakā and Rambhā and the other *apsaras*es develop the theme with poetic embellishment.[32]

Abiśaptā Urvaśī

The *Abhiśapta Urvaśī*,[33] a play in Assamese which consists of three acts, is by Narayana Kataky,[34] a playwright. It is based on the story originally found in the *Ṛgveda* and Purāṇas. It may be assumed that this immortal legend has influenced many poets and dramatists throughout the ages to depict the theme in various novel styles. Thus, such a play has been handed down to us.

The theme of the play in question, i.e., the *Abhiśapta Urvaśī*, is described briefly as follows.

Urvaśī, the celestial dancer, is shown in heaven which is ruled by Indra. Here she commits an offence in the presence of Durvāsā, a mighty and angry sage, who desired to enjoy celestial dance performance in the *svargaloka*. Urvaśī expresses excessive hatred and negligence out of pride, and when the sage comes to know of her vanity he curses her to go to the mortal world transformed into a mare. However, Indra comes to the rescue and gives an alternative way: that she would remain in the form of mare in broad daylight and in the night she would get transformed into a woman, and when the eight kinds of missiles (*aśtravajras*) would be united in the battle-field she would be released in no time.

The second Act starts with the fatigued king Daṇḍin, ruler of Avantī, who runs after a wonderful mare in the dense forest. He is surprised to find in the evening, that the mare has regained her celestial form of an *apsarā*. She discloses her actual identity before the king and the latter is charmed with her beauty and takes her to his capital as his wife.

The third Act begins with a conversation of Kṛṣṇa with his attendants in the Court of Dvārakā, and Nārada informing that the mare possessed by Daṇḍin should belong to Kṛṣṇa. Accordingly, out of curiosity, Kṛṣṇa sends Sātyakī to Daṇḍin. However, the proposal sends by Kṛṣṇa enrages Daṇḍin, and out of pride he replies that he would never surrender to Kṛṣṇa the mare he possesses. Kṛṣṇa declares war against Daṇḍin. Helpless, Daṇḍin and Urvaśī make up their minds to jump into the river Gaṅgā but Subhadrā's (sister of Kṛṣṇa and wife of Arjuna) presence saves them from death. She also assures him that she would help him at the cost of her own life if necessary. She calls upon Bhīma, couregeous elder brother of Arjuna along with Arjuna and the other brothers to stand against Kṛṣṇa's unholy demand. Although the Pāṇḍavas are at a loss to know what to do at the very outset they do not desist from the path of morality and *dharma*. Kṛṣṇa stands against them along with a huge army including Śiva, Indra and Yama. All the hostile parties are standing in their respective places and the battle begins. When all the invincible missiles are fixed to be shot at each other by the famous heroes, all of a sudden Urvaśī discards her mortal mare form, asssumes her celestial beauty and flies away. Indra then discloses all the past events relating to the curse of Durvāsas for which Urvaśī had to suffer a wretched life in the mortal world. Kṛṣṇa declares with that this story would be a message and ideal of encouragement for the later generations.

References

1. Dipak Chandra, Deys Publishing, Calcutta, 1988.
2. Dipak Chandra has written a good number of novels relating to the episodes of the *Rām* and *Mbh*, where he has revealed his creative ability through imagination and fanciful stories.
3. Read, *Urvaśī Jananī*, p. 14.
   urvaśī mahāpuruṣa nārāyaner aurasajata santāna
4. Cp. *Mbh*. 1
   Vide *Urvaśī Jananī*, p. 10.
5. *Urvaśī Jananī*, pp. 28-9.
   'Daityaraj Keśin caya to make'.
6. *Ibid*., p. 36:
   gandharva rajyer narapati viśvāvasu indrer
   sahāya niye kumār vane sainya samavesa karese
7. *Ibid*., p. 37:
   indra caya urvaśī ke tar prati indrer durbalatā purūravar ajana nāy
   Also: *tamāke pete caya amar sav sampader binimaye*
8. *Ibid*., p. 64:
   sabar theke bhālbasi āmar svadesake mātṛbhūmike
9. Vide p. 65:
   putra āyu, rajir janyei tār ekhan thākar dārkar

10. *Ibid.*, p. 69:

    bibāh mane vandijivan, bibāḥ mane svathaparata, bibah hal śarīr upabhager adhikār.

11 *Ibid.*, p. 110:

    kāraṇa mitra o varuṇa ubhayei urvaśī ke mane-mane kāmana kare

12. *Ibid.*, p. 146:

    amarāvatite tṛtiya pandava arjuner agaman ghatala

    Ibid., p. 150:

    kṛṣṇai hayata arjuna ke pathiyeche.

13. *Ibid.*, p. 168 *'sraddha haya'*

    Ibid., p. 170:

    devi amake aparadhi kar na. tamake ami satyi sraddha kari. bhīṣan śraddhā kāri.

14. *Ibid.*, p. 183: *bhul sav manuser hay. kintu sab nārī urvaśī hāi na. urvaśī ekajanai hay.*

    cetanar bhetar theke arjuner mātā daktā hātat tar bhitare gam gam kare uthala.

    p. 186, *ratha cutal pretisthan parer dike*

15. Read Bhramar Ramkumar. Kaurava-Pāṇḍava par ādhārit upanyāsa — Adhikār Ārambha Adhikār Asādhya Aṅkan Āvāhan Āhuti, etc. Hind Pocket Books Pvt. Ltd.

16. Dinakar was born on 29th September in 1908. He has written a good number of books and epics in Hindī language, and, thus, enriched the store of Hindī literature.

17. Publisher Uayacal Rastrakavi Dinakar Path Rajendranagar, Patna Edition, September, 1986.

18. Read Urvaśī 1, 23

    sādha! sādha! menakā! tumhāra bhi man kahi phanca hain
    mittikā mohan kavi antar mein jan bācā hain ॥

    ....*urvaśī keśī ki*

    sakhi urvaśī si tum bhi lagti-sukusca madmati he ।
    martya ek mahimā tum bhi ta usi taraḥ gati hi ॥

19. *Ibid.*, 1.23-4:

    nahin jāti he ke ek din ham kaber ke ghar se ।
    tata lubdhva syen sa hamki tras aparimit dekar
    aur turat uda jaya urvaśī ki bahun mein lekar ॥

20. *Ibid.*, 1, 26:

    ham tu hain apsarā pavan mein mukta biharanevālī ।
    gita-nāda sanmah-subasa se sav ki bharnavali ।

apna hain abas, na jane kitri ki caha main ।
kaise ham bandha rahen kisi bhi nar ka da bahun main ।।

21. *Ibid.*, 2, 45:

tav bhi marut anukul hin
mujki milen ja sala hin,
priyatam jahan bhi hin sisce-
savarta path main phool hein ।।

22. Read 3, 48, 66:

surapati tar tak hi savadhan rahte bah kar apnane ki ।
apsarā svarga se ati hain andhariaka cumbona pane ki ।।

23. *bhārat śāpa jitna bhi katu tha ab tak avh bar hit tha* ।
uskā dahak rupa sakanege av arambha huwa hein ।।

24. *Ibid.*, 4, 98-118:

asca ta a gayi citralekhe
kahan bandhane ki priya ke alingan mein ।।

25. *Ibid.*, 5, 135-6:

aaila vamsa ka mukut aya the mastak par dharta haw ।
mahārāj ।
me bhar-mukta ava kanan ki jatā hun ।।

han mein abhi rajmahisi thi cahe jahan kahi bhi ।।

Vide *Vikramorvaśīyam* of Kālidāsa, Act 5, pp. 232 edited M.R. Kale 'Bhāgavata Cyavarana Sesaman usthtam'.

26. *Ibid.*, 1., 23-24

pukar hamari sum eka rāja he
daor pade ve sadaja urvaśī kiabilanba bacane ।
mukta hui urvaśī hamari ens din kal kabal se ।।

27. Read, the *Vikramorvaśīyam* of Kālidāsa, Act 2, p. 82, M.R. Kale, 1967:

anjya trapsmi devya kasirajputya yatha
hanji nipanike yataḥ prabhiti
bhagabatah surjysyaprasthanam krtva
pratinivrttha ayuatrastata arambhya
sunadhrdaya eva laksyate ।।

28. Read *Śak.* Kālidāsa — Act. IV, 18

bhartuviprakrtapi rasanataya masma pratipam gamaḥ ।।

Ibid., I Act VI

Ibid., 2, 45:

apsara ke saiga ramana isa ku aradhana hai ।
patrapane ke liye bihara kare va kunja van me

aur main aradhana karte rahu sune bhaven me.

Vide *Vikramorvaśīyam*, Act 2, p. 132:

ma khalu laghuhrdyaham anushayam baha manye

Read Notes p. 325

Edition, M.R. Kale, 1967

29. *Ibid.*, 4, 116, p.

'bhārat śāp dussaha duranta kitna katu dukhadayi hain ।

Vide — *The Vikramorvaśīyam*, Act. 3, p. 138:

yena mamupadesasstvaya lanjuitaistena na te
divyam ṣṭḥānm bhabisyatīntyupādhāyasya śāpḥ ।।

Vide *The Śākuntalam*, Act. 4, 1.

30. Read — *The Vikramorvaśīyam*, Act 3, p. 138

mahendreṇa punaḥ Prekṣybasānam eajjā Vantamukhī bhaṇitā.

Act 5, p. 250:

trikaladarsibhimunibhiradistah ....

31. *Ibid.*, 5, 120-2:

svapna hi kaha yadapi
cyavanasrama ke pas palama ki
dragambu dhara si.

Vide B.C.

32. *Ibid.*, 5, 135:

mein bhar mukta ab kana kujata hein

Vide — *The Vikramorvaśīyam*, Act. 5, p. 250

33. Read — *Urvaśī*, Dinakar, p.8

34. *Ibid.*, pp. 21-22-23

Read also Agarwal Maya, *Urvaśī EK Vivecana* 'Bhumika', Anita Prakasan, Delhi, 1969.

6

Urvaśī and Devadāsīs

THE foregoing chapters have attempted to give a clear picture of the origin and development of the institution of the *apsaras*es and their role in Indian culture, and the legend of Urvaśī and Purūravas in particular. From the accounts studied, it appears that the institution of the *apsaras*es laid the foundation of the age-old tradition of another allied institution — that of the *devadāsī*s. The ancient literature gives us enough testimony to the origin of Indian dance side by side with the growth of drama and music. Numerous allusions in the texts repeatedly say how the *apsaras*es had taken part in the gay celebration of festivals. Even the *Rām*[1] bears evidence that the sage Bharadvāja held a great reception ceremony in honour of Bharata, the prince of Ayodhyā, where the host of *apsaras*es presented a series of dance performances at the command of the sage. Indra is said to have owned a harem full of *apsaras*es, who usually presented dance and music in his court in honour of the gods and sages. The word *devadāsī*,[2] meaning servant/maid-servant/maid-servant of god, hints that such was the origin of the institution. The *apsaras*es were nothing but the concubines of heaven. They were never married to the gods; rather they served as the female-partners in the sensuous enjoyment enjoyed by the gods. These *apsaras*es are said to have played some role even in the enactment plays first introduced by Bharata.[3]

Scholars like Prajesh Banerjee opine that the *devadāsī*s[4] have close affinity with the *apsaras*es in their mode of living, worship and ideals. They claim that they have inherited the arts of dance from the *apsaras*es and they are their daughters. It is well known that the art of dancing was practised by the *devadāsī*s and the origin of all the classical dances of India, viz., Bharat Nāṭyam, Kathakalī, Oḍissī, Maṇipurī and Kathak is linked with them. There is a legend associated with king Indradyumna who erected the Jagannātha temple at Purī (Utkal). It is said that the *apsaras*es and the *gandharva*s came there with Brahmā and Viśvakarman to attend the function. The dance of Urvaśī and Rambhā enhanced the splendour of the function along with the music of the *gandharva*s. Urvaśī who danced in the Court of Indra and attended several functions held in the mortal world (*Mbh*) is said to have borne the germ of the *devadāsī*s of the later period. Therefore, Urvaśī was a *devadāsī*.[5] And it is said that from that time onwards the tradition of dancing in the temples before gods started. The *devadāsī*s of Purī were known as *maharī*s. The derivative name of the word *devadāsī* is found in the lexicography as follows: *Deva-devas-god*s. *Dāsi*s means slaves, slave of gods, i.e., those who remained as the slaves or consorts of the gods. Gods were pleased ten times with dance and music with eulogy'. A *devadāsī* was servant or attendant upon a temple; a female in the service of gods or temples; a courtesan employed as a dancer in a temple.[6]

It is stated that three stages of the institution of *devadāsī* were in vogue in the early period. In the first stage, the *devadāsī*s were regarded as consorts of the deity of the temples. They used to please the presiding deity with the art of music and dance. They were reserved for the deity only. But in the second stage, the *devadāsī*s had to dedicate their lives to the cause of the gods as desired by the brāhmaṇa priests who were prominent by birth in the society and who were thought to be the representatives of the deity. In the third stage, they were forced to satisfy the lust of the common men who often visited the place of pilgrimage. They became courtesans in course of time.

Temples and devadāsīs

From the ancient period of time temples have been built by the Hindus in order to worship their deities. Some persons were appointed in the temples to devote themselves to their upkeep through activities like the placing of idols, giving them a bath, collecting flowers for worshipping the deity and cleaning the courtyard and the altar of the temples.

A large number of girls (virgins) of full youth and beauty were appointed for dancing and music and they were trained under the guidance of expert *gurus*. It was a belief at that time that the gods may be pacified and pleased through dance and music which are connected with the eulogy and glorification of gods established in the temple. Instances are available to show that the temples were the abode of the *devadāsīs* and courtesans. In the *Meghadūta* of Kālidāsa,[7] a *devadāsī* performs dance before the idol of Śiva (Mahākāla) located at Ujjayinī.

Dance and music — particularly the classical dances — are associated with temples established by devotees in India. The religious-minded Hindus were interested in busying themselves in enjoyment of dancing, music and dramatic performances. In India every month or season is observed with the celebration of festivals and ceremonies which feature various kinds of dance and music. The *Holī*, the *Rāsalīlā* (*pūrṇimā*), the *Vijaya Daśamī* (Dasara), the *Vasantotsava* and so on are celebrated in utmost joy. The Hindus are by nature fond of festivals. As the poet Kālidāsa said, "All men are fond of festivals."[8]

So dancing girls were hereditarily attached to temples and dance must have formed a regular feature of the temple ritual. Instances of appointment of the *devadāsīs* for religious purposes are found abundantly. Dancing was prescribed on the occasion of the awakening of the gods, for instance, to rouse Viṣṇu from his sleep, the lord Śiva on the *caturdaśī* day (of the Phālguna), on their birth anniversaries, and on other occasions related to their worship, such as at the time of installation of divine images, or on the arrival of a new season or the advent of harvest festivals, i.e., on the occasion of gathering corn or fruits.

Kalhaṇa, the author of *Rājataraṅginī*[9] of Kashmir not only refers to the association of dancing girls with temples but also speaks of the personal interest shown by some kings towards this tradition. Kalasa had the hobby of collecting dancing girls. King Harṣa personally instructed dancing girls on the art of acting and music.

It goes without saying that the temples were the main centres of music and dance in ancient India. Every important temple had its *mandir* hall of dance and music. Evidence of the inscriptions says that womenfolk of the temples were originally dedicated to gods. The Bhubaneswar inscription asserts that a lady named Kalāvatī with some other beautiful women adorned with ornaments set in gems were dedicated to Lord Śiva.[10]

Again south-Indian inscriptions dated AD 1153 refer to the grant of land for the worship of god and maintenance of dancing girls. The origin of this custom may be traced to the need for good music at the time of worship of gods and popular festivals. Besides, the dancing girls in the temple were also called Gudisani.

In comparison to the temples located in northern India, the south-Indian temples, especially the Śiva temples, were mostly the centres of the *devadāsī* custom. These temples gave constant employment to a number of priests, charioteers, musicians, dancing girls, florists, cooks, and other classes of servants.

> Hereafter temples ascertain abbeys in which gods, and goddesses to whom many young girls are consecrated *devadāsī*s (Marcopole).[11]

Dance was then used to please the gods in the temples and

shrines. The dance performed in temples had a religious sentiment to it. Through generations, this *devadāsī* tradition continued and the profession of dance was preserved for the girls in temples. References are made to the theatre and dances in shrines in the inscriptions of Rājarāja and other Cola kings of the Tanjore district in the eleventh century.

Citrāṅgadā

It is stated that Citrāṅgadā,[12] wife of Arjuna, was a *devadāsī* or she might have belonged to a family of *devadāsī*s. *Devadāsī*s were looked down upon in the higher society and, therefore, she was not taken to Hastināpura after marriage. Such a question of dignity exists even now. Adequate examples can be cited in this regard, which are available in the provincial versions of the *Mbh* (the *Mbh* in Bengali and Assamese, for instance).

In the bosom of the caves of Yagimāra[13] and Sītābaṅga near Rāmgiri hill in the district of Madhya Pradesh, an inscription has been discovered carved on stone with an illustration in which a troop of *devadāsī*s are depicted along with the *apsarases*, *gandharvas* and with the musical party. The meaning of the inscription is obtained through the poem translated by revered *paṇḍita* Vyāsrāj and also a prose interpretation which are given below:

> Poets, the leaders of lovers
> High up the hearts which are heavy with passion
> She who rides on a seashore
> the object of jest and blame
> how can she have fallen so deep in love

Sutanukā by name, a *devadāsī*. The excellent among men loved her — *Devadinna* by name, skilled in sculpture.

> Sutanukā the slave girl (*devadāsikiya*) of the Gods
> loved the excellent young man Devadatta by name.

Devadāsī: Profession prevailed in Kerala

In India the *devadāsī* system has a very ancient history and tradition which can be traced back to many centuries ago. Most of the classical dances of today owe their origin to the temple. Dancers were known as Dāsīyattam. Although the Greek name hepo 'devesoi' means temple dancing girls, it would be far-fetched to claim that the *devadāsī* tradition in India was introduced by the Western civilisation.

In Kerala *devadāsī*s[14] came to be known as *Tevadiche* which means 'servants of God'. In the early years of *devadāsī* tradition, dances were performed by women of the royal and noble families, because the offerings were made to the supreme lord who demanded the obeisance of women of the highest social and cultural status. It is believed that the Chera king Kulaśekhara Alwar himself offered his daughter (Andal) as a *devadāsī* to the Lord of the Temple of Śrīraṅgam. The *devadāsī* was confined to the temple precinct. These *jevedigal*s were trained in the family tradition and, hence, became a class known as *Tevedian*.

A detailed description of the *devadāsī*s can be had in K.K. Pillai's *The Sachasdarm Temple*.

More information and investigation[15] on the *devadāsī* tradition which prevailed during the early and middle period of India may be discussed as indicated below.

It is said that sometimes some unwealthy fathers/ guardians had to sell their girls to the wealthy priests of some temples in exchange for pecuniary gain. One of the chief grounds was that some poverty-stricken guardians could not bear the expenditure of marriage of daughters and the possibility was that they had to remain unmarried in life for good. So they were sent to the temple and they practised dance, learnt to sing, and acquired other musical qualifications. After attainment of puberty they became prey to the lustful priests, who thought themselves to be representatives or incarnations of god, sword, *triśūla* among others, to which the girls were wedded. They were forced to have intercourse with the priests or with other persons — influential persons of the society or persons associated with the temples. The offsprings they gave birth to were renowned as *devadāsīs* or slaves of gods in the later period.

Servants: Such kinds of girls or virgins were kept in the temples for external duties like collecting flowers and cleaning the temples both inside and outside. In spite of their low birth, if they could possess beauty they could never get rid of the lust of the priests and others. They were to dedicate their youth to the lustful persons.

Bhaktā: Such type of maidens were forsaken by their husbands and their near and dear ones and they had to ask for protection in the temples. They were called nuns. Of course, they never dedicated their lives to lustful persons.

Duttā: Such type of girls were dedicated by their parents' desire. A legend goes to state that one Padmāvatī was sent by her parents to the Jagannātha temple to become a *devadāsī*. But the parents had a wonderful dream where they were advised that Padmāvatī should be wedded to Jayadeva, who was a true devotee of Lord Jagannātha. And accordingly Padmāvatī was wedded to Jayadeva and she became renowned as a *devadāsī*.

Evidence of devadāsīs and Śiva temples

The cult of *devadāsī* was in vogue in all the temples of India. It is to be noted that especially the Śiva temples were centres of *devadāsī* culture. With reference to this point we may mention the Hājo temple, Viśvanātha temple (Assam) located in the Śonitpur district and the famous Śiva temple of Dergāon (District Jorhāṭ). In the Dergāon Śiva temple (which is renowned as the Śiva temple of Negheriting, Dergāon) a good number of girls danced before the idol of Śiva in days of old, especially during the Āhom period. The Āhom kings highly patronised this cult: they donated land and money lavishly for spreading the sacred tradition.[16]

A legend goes to state that in ancient time Urvaśī, the foremost of the *apsaras*es, had to exhibit her attractive dance in the Court of Indra, Lord of the gods. In that function Śiva was one of the chief spectators among other gods. During her dance she (Urvaśī) cast her side-glances at Śiva and harboured deep love towards him to attain him as a husband. She proceeded to Kailāsa, the abode of Śiva and made a unique attempt to break his penance through her marvellous dance and song. The penance was disturbed, but unfortunately a curse was hurled on her by Śiva. Being propitiated through austere devotion Śiva forgave her with the condition that she should dance at a stretch at the temple of Kāmrūpa where Śiva resides. From that time onwards the system of *devadāsī*s started in the Śiva temples, the abode of Śiva. The Śiva temple became famous as Parihareśvar Devālaya in course of time. Whether Urvaśī could fulfil her desire of attaining Śiva as her husband or not, the legend is still prevalent among the Śiva *bhakta*s.[17]

It is believed that some of the heavenly *apsaras*es who came to the mortal world on occasions became mortal queens like Urvaśī and spread the germ of dance and song. We may assume that Urvaśī, the divine damsel and divine courtesan, was originally a *devadāsī*.[18]

Devadāsī and Śaṅkaradeva

Although it is said time and again that the *devadāsī* cult prevailed mostly in the Śiva temples, it gained popularity in every nook and corner of India and was in existence in some of the Vaiṣṇava temples also. It is said that when Śaṅkaradeva, a great saint of Assam (1440-1569), paid a visit to the holy place of Jagannātha during his long tour of India, he happened to witness the *devadāsī* dance and was spellbound.[19]

Yoginī Tantra and devadāsī

The *Yogini Tantra* and *Kālikā Purāṇa* bear evidence that the tradition of *devadāsī* flourished even before the Āryan culture came to prevail in Assam. During the rule of the *kirātas*, Śiva was worshipped as their chief deity and the dances of *devadāsī*s were presented before the idol of Śiva.[20]

It is said that in the temple called Hāṭakeśvara near Tezpur (Assam) the tradition of *devadāsī*s was in vogue and the *devadāsī*s were known as *devāṅganā* (women of the temple).

Banamāladeva, the king of Kāmarūpa, himself rebuilt the temple of Hāṭakeśvara (Śiva), where he dedicated a number of girls (dancers) for dancing. This system still persists in the Śiva temple of Hājo and Dubi in Kāmarūp district (now in the District of Kāmarūpa and Bārpeṭā) and in the Negheriting (Dergāon) temple.

The *devadāsī*s of the temples located in Āssam were called *naṭ*, courtesans. Generally they were renowned as temple dancers.[21]

Temple women or prostitution is reported to have been prevalent in all periods of Assam's history. The Śiva temples located in Assam were highly noted for two reasons — one of them was the tradition of *devadāsī*s, who were known as the *naṭī* and who danced regularly. And another feature was that in the Śiva temple located at Dergāon, the goats were strangled to death in the temple.[22]

Āhom queen Phūleśvarī was originally a devadāsī

It has been already said that the dancing girls who belonged to the Śiva temple were born as *devadāsī*s and were brought up in that tradition. Phūlmatī, who became queen Phūleśvarī,[23] wife of Śiva Singh, was originally a *devadāsī* or *naṭī* by birth. Once the king had a chance to witness her dance performance in the Śiva temple on the occasion of *Durgā-pūjā* in the month of Āśvina. The king was enamoured with her exquisite beauty and excellent dance performance. He immediately brought her to the harem and married her with due rites of the Āhom tradition and customs.

The origin of Bharat Nāṭyam

The famous dance Bharat Nāṭyam[24] is known to have developed as a *devadāsī nṛtya*. Before it was standardised it was a vulgar one, and considered as immoral and looked down upon. But by the efforts of Śrīkṛṣṇa Āyar, the dance was developed. Rukmiṇī Devī saved this *nṛtya* from threatened ruin and oblivion and helped it to attain the present popularity and international reputation. In fact, the rules of Bharat Nāṭyam have become part of the history of Indian classical dance.

Mādhava Kandalī's Rāmāyaṇa

The tradition of *devadāsī* was looked down upon in the society[25] during the time of Mādhava Kandalī who was the best poet of the pre-Śaṅkaradeva age and who brought out the *Rāmāyaṇa* (Sanskrit) in Assamese language. In his version of the epic, he says, "After the destruction of Rāvaṇa, Sitā was freed and she was asked to prove her chastity before Rāma and his attendants. Then being humiliated Sītā retorted that she was being treated as a *naṭī*." This version has a parallel in the *Rāmāyaṇa* of Vālmīki.[26]

Devadāsī: A holy tradition

The *devadāsī* tradition was seen as an inferior one by the upper classes in India. But some parts of the world, particularly Greece, America, Mesopotamia and Libya, join to offer honour to this tradition. This tradition is found to be in vogue in families located around the coast of Malabar and in some places of Tamil Nadu in India where it is being maintained with an effort. From the ancient time this tradition has prevailed in the temples of Hājo and Dubi in Kāmrūpa district.

Devadāsī: Social evils and Indian women

Forced prostitution[28] in the name of God perpetrated by anti-social elements has grown to be another social evil. Instances of this practice can be found to be growing in some parts of the State of Karnataka and other States where the *devadāsī* system is still prevailing. The system was banned by the Government but it is of no avail. Girls mainly from backward classes and castes of the society are forced to marry the gods in temples. They are to serve in the temple and are called *devadāsīs*. But in reality they are forced to fulfil the lust of the landlords and rich people who belong to villages. These *devadāsīs* are deprived of a conjugal life, and they are called 'Khaṇḍabhogavatī' as their marriage is in fact never coming. This system flourished under the Colas and Pallavas. It is said that such women in Kerala are not allowed to cover the upper part of their body, and they are not allowed to wear clean clothes, as clean clothes are the prerogative of the upper class of women. And it is a fact that these girls are abducted and sold in the famous red-light zones of Marana and Bhiṇḍ of Madhya Pradesh for illicit purposes.

The inhabitants of the red light areas of metropolitan cities have borne out this truth.

Devadāsī : Source hailed from Western countries

Scholars of repute are in a dilemma in forwarding opinions with regard to this tradition. But some scholars opine that this tradition hailed from the inner parts of the Mediterranean sea.[29] It is described that, there the maidens before their marriage were dedicated to dance in the temples. The temples of Egypt were full of such *devadāsīs*. This tradition was in vogue within the families of the Hebrews and Babylonians. And, thus, it was influenced by the non-Āryan society where Śiva's position was upgraded. Along with his worship, dance performed by the *devadāsīs* for his interest prevailed in the Āryan society and families. The post-Vedic literature, especially the *Padma Purāṇa* and the *Bhaviṣya Purāṇa*, bear evidence in this connection. It is described that there were about four hundred *devadāsīs* in Tanjore. The *devadāsīs* belonging to Maharashtra were 'Muruli' by name and those who belonged to Andhra were 'Bṛṣabhī' by name. And it is said that in the temple of Somanātha there were five hundred *devadāsīs* during the invasion of Sultān Mahmud.[30]

Although this *devadāsī* dance or tradition is now in vogue in many parts including Assam,[31] we may still take pride that this lost glory of our culture has been restored through tremendous efforts and interest of some scholars of Assam whom we cannot ignore at all. They were late Biṣṇu Prasad Rābhā, Suresh Gośwāmī, Dr. Moheśwar Neog and Late R.K. Tālukdār among others. They have tried the utmost to preserve and restore it with and this neglected tradition has come to gain royal recognition from the Central Government with the courtesy of the Information and Broadcasting Department of India from 1964.

From the discussion of origin and development of the *devadāsī* dance and the cult it now appears to us that the germ of the tradition was latent in the tradition of the *apsarases*. The *apasarases* were *devadāsīs* of an earlier time. Later the *devadāsīs* became a regular feature in the temple.

The Vedic Indians were also fond of *soma* and women. It is said that girls without brothers were frequently reduced to prostitution. Instances of such free trade women were not rare in ancient India.[32]

The *VisP* refers to the institution of the prostitute in connection with royal consecration. Pichel saw many references to harlots in the *Ṛgveda*. Uṣas is likened to a dancing girl wearing embroidered garments and baring her bosom. They are referred to as courtesans and as the associates of the Maruts. And according to Weber these were unchaste women in the Vedic age. In the Vrātyakāṇḍa of the *AV* reference is made to the unchaste women, *pāncalis*.

Thus, one can conclude that the institution of the *devadāsīs* followed the pattern of the service rendered to gods by the *apsarases* in the remote age. No *apsarā* was allowed to marry a single person and they had to remain as the permanent common women for any one. This is true of the *devadāsīs* too. They were to marry the idol of the temple and remain attached to the temple. But their youth and beauty were subjected to the lust of the persons around the temple, particularly the rich men.

References

1. Read Rām, 2, 91, 16-17, 47

   āhvaye devagandharvān viśvāvasu-hā-hāhuhun ।
   tathaivāpsaraso devagandharvaścāipi sarvaśaḥ ।। 16 ।।

   ghṛtācimathaviśvācimmiśrakeśīmalambuṣām ।
   nagadattām ca heman hemāmad kṛtāsthalim ।। 17 ।।

   alambuṣā miśrakeśī puṇḍarikātha vāmana ।। 46 ।।

2. Read Apte V.M., p. 256: *The Students' Sanskrit and English Dictionary* specifies the following meanings (1) Servants or attendants upon a temple, (2) A female in the sacrifice of gods or the temple, (3) Courtesan employed as a dancer in the temple.

3. Bharata's *Nāṭyaśāstra* 1. 46-47:

   āśākyā puruṣaih sādhu prayuktam strīnādṛte
   tatashsṛgan mahatejā manasahaspārasa bibhaḥ

   mañjukeśīm, sokeśīm, ca miśrkeśī sulacanām
   sandāminīm devaduttām devasenām manaramā ।।

   sadatīm sundarīm caiva vidaghām vivadhām tathā
   sumalām, santatīm caiva sunandām, sumukhīm tathā

   mājadhīm mārjunīm caiva saralām keralām dhṛtīm ।।
   nandām, supaskalām, caiva kalabhām, caiva medadan ।।

   Read also Keith A.B., *A History of Sanskeit Drama*.

4. Read Banerjee, *Apsaras in Indian Dance*, New Delhi 1982, p. 115.

5. Banerjee, P., *The Devadāsī Cult*. 'Basic concepts of Indian Dance', New Delhi, 1987, pp. 10-16.

   Vide Śrīpantha : *Devadāsī Ānandabājār Patrikā* (*Bengālī*) *Śāradiya*, 1372, Calcutta, p. 264.

Urvaśī, Menakā, Rambhā — Sargvalaker sei sundarira ki sudhu nartakī mātra sila'.

6. Read Bardoloi, Pavan 'Udasi nṛttyar bicār, Gutipa nṛttya Natun Ranghar, January 94, pp. 11-12, Guwahati.
7. Read *Meghadūta* 1, 35 Pūrvamegha

   pādanyāsaikvantasvastatra lilabadhutai ।
   ratacsaya khasitabali bhiscamaraih klāntahasta ।

   veśyāstata nakhapadasukhan prāpya varsagha binda
   namaksyante tvayi madhukarasti nidirghan kataksaya ।।
8. Read Kālidāsa *Abhijñāna-Śakuntalam* Act. 6 *Utssaba Khala*..........

   Read also Gupta, Dāmodar, *Kuṭṭnimatta*, Motilal Banarsidass, p. 224, Vide Banerjee, P., *Apsaras in Inidan Dance*, p. 30
9. Vide *Śrīpantha Devadāsī*, p. 262

   aṣtam śatake rājataranjani sākhya kāśmira devadāsī āse.

   Vide Chaudhuri, Satish Ch., 'Sanskritir Subās' *Pāthśālā Sāhitya Sabha*, 1987, p. 11.

   Vide 'Banjali Darpaṇ', *Smritigranṭha* edited by B. Śarmā, Dhiren Tālukdār, Pāthśāla, 1977, p. 129.
10. Banerjee, Anil Chandra, *History of India*, Calcutta, 1973, p. 148.
11. Read Śāstri, K.A. Nīlakānta, *A History of South India*, 1966, p. 324.

    Vide *Śrīpantha-Devadāsī*, p. 262

    tārek tāmraśāsaner baktabya rājarāja-tāniorer mandira saśikṣitā cārsa telesseri pendugal ba mandir kanyā dānkaresen; Vide Banerjee, P., *Apsarases in Indian Dance*, p. 96.
12. Read Dutta Baruah, Harinārāyan, ed. (Assamese) *Mahābhārat*, Pāthśālā, Assam, 1955, I, p. 141.

    citrāṇgadā nāme mai jewigandharvar ।
    patikāma phuru moi vanar bhitar ।।

    tamāka barilu śvāmī nakara nairākha ।
    yaciyā tamāt kaila patihābilākha ।।
13. Read Choudhury, Satish Ch., 'Devadāsī nṛtya Paramparā' *Sanskritir Subāsa*, Pāthśāla, 1987, p. 10, Vide Sānyal Nārāyan, *Sutanukā kan devadāsīr nām nay*, Calcutta, 1992, p. 35.

    Vide *Śrīpanth-Devadāsī*, p. 277, Vide Chaliha, P., 'Asamar Mandirar Śeṣar Adhyāya', *Adhināyaka*, 1st-10th November, 1989, pp. 7-45, Guwahāti.
14. Read Bhāratī, Śhivājī, *The Art of Mahinyāttam*, New Delhi, 1986, p. 15.
15. Read *Śrīpanthạ-Devadāsī*, p. 275, Vide Banerjee, P. *Apsaras in Indian*

Dance, p. 116, Vide Chaudhuri, Satish Ch., 'Devadāsī nṛtyar paramparā', *Sanskritir Subhāsh*, Pāthśālā, 1987, p. 11.

16. Read Kalita, Trikendranath, '*Dubi Devālyar Luptapraya Devadāsī nṛtya, Dainik Janambhumi*, Jorhat, Sunday, October 6, 1991; Also *ibid.*, *Dubir Devadāsī* Vide Banerjee, P., *Apsaras in Indian Dance*, p. 133: "When the followers of Śiva worship Him in dance or when the *devadāsī* dances round the image on the God enshrined in the temple, it is the divine dancer who is their inspiration and with his created mode, they express their adoration which results in self-forgetfulness."

    Vide, Chauduri, Satish Chandra, 'Devadāsī nṛtyar Paramparā' *Sanskritir Subāsa*, Pāthśālā, 1987, p. 13. Vide, Deva Choudhury, *Paresh, Devadāsī nṛttya Chandaśilpa*, 4th July, 1991, pp. 19-20.

    Vide Baruāh, B.K. *Asamar Lokasanskriti*, Lawyers' Book Stall, Guwāhāti, 1961, p. 113.

    "The *devadāsīnṛtya* of Assam was attached to the worship and ritual activities belonging to the gods and goddesses. . . . This dance was related to the dance of the southern India; especially this dance was practised in the shrine of the Śaiva and Śākta temples in India." Vide, Dās, Prabin Ch. *Panyabhumī Hājo*, Guwahati, Assam Rupa Prakāsh, 1983, pp. 47-8.

17. Read Baruah Tultul, '*Devadāsī nṛtyar Ādi Parvan* (Article), *Dainik Janambhumi*, Jorhat, 29th year, No. 166, 18 Nov. 1990.

18. Read also, Banerjee, P., *Basic Concepts of Indian Dance, The Devadāsī Cult*, New Delhi, 1987, pp. 10-16.

19. Read Lekhāru Upendranāth, ed., *Kathāgurucarita*, Nalbāri, 1952, p. 155 '*dāsī nācice etar kalbin (upperjarment) khahice*'

20. Read, Neog Maheśwar, *Puraṇi Asamiyā Samāj āru Sanskriti*, New Book Stall, Guwahati, Vide Barooah K.K., *Early History of Kāmarūp*, Guwāhāti, 1966, p. 78.

21. Read Choudhurī, Satish, *Sanskritir Subāsh*, Pāthśāla Guwahati, 187, p. 11.

22 Read Borthākur, Guṇeśwar, *The History of Negheriting and Śhiva Religions*, 1st edn., Guwahati, 1979, p. 15.

23. Read, Barrūāh Hiteśwar, *Āhomar Din*, Āssam Prakāśan Pariṣad, Guwahati, 1981, p. 243.

24. Read 'The Origin of Bhārat Nātyam', *Bhavan's Journal*, vol. XXVII, No. 25, July 9, 1972.

25. Read Chutia Mukut Singh, 'Āntarjātik Nari āru āmi', *Natun Dainik*, Assamese Daily, Guwahati 8th March, 1991.

26. Vide Kandali Mādhav (Assamese) *Rāmāyaṇa* 6, 6508. op. 449,

āmak itar nāri same dekhilāhā
naṭor naṭini yena āmak bilāhā ।।

27. Read '*Kāmrūpa*', Kāmrūpa Sāhitya Pariṣad ed. by Rām Charan Thākuriā, 4th session, 1975.
28. Devī Praṇati, 'The Gauhāti University Times' 16th yr., May 1988 Issue No. 1.
29. Read, Chaudhury Satish Ch., *Sanskritir Subāsa*, Pāthśālā, Sāhitya Sabha, 12th Feb., 1987, p. 10.
30. Sripantha, Calcutta, 1392, pp. 257-62.
31. Read, Śāstri K.A. Nilalkānta, *A History of South India*, 1966, pp. 32-5.
32. Read Chaudhury, Satish Ch., *Sanskritir Subāsa*, 1967, pp. 18-29.

7

Conclusion

In the foregoing chapters of this work we have dealt with the origin, nature and status of *apsaras*es in Indian mythology and the legend of Purūravas and Urvaśī in particular in great detail. In the course of our study we have made certain observations, particularly at the end of each section. Now it is time to draw conclusions on the basis of the study as a whole.

Efforts have been made to look into the origin and characteristics of the *apsaras*es in the background of the Indo-European mythology (ch. 2). The emphasis is on Greek mythology which identifies some and creatures as nymphs and classifies them as those relates to water, those living in lonely graves.

Coming to Indian mythology one has to plunge into a deep and vast literature to trace the origin and development of the *apsaras*es. They are said to have been born of one Prādhā who was married to Kāśyapa. She was a daughter of Dakṣa Prajāpati, and, thus, she was a sister of Aditi and Diti. A majority of the prominent *apsaras*es were born of her. These *apsaras*es influenced the lives of the gods, *asura*s, men-sages and kings. Gods indulged in sexual enjoyment with them. They did not intend to marry any of them and did not give them the status of a married wife. They were kept as *sādhāraṇa strī*, 'concubine'. Therefore, chastity was a word not to be associated to them. But Urvaśī, the foremost of the *apsaras*es, is known to have been born in an artificial way. She was born from the thigh of Lord Nārāyaṇa, the primeval sage. Then she was presented to Indra as a gift.

Indra, the lord of the gods, used them as an efficient weapon to reap benefit out of their forms and traits. Often they were commanded or sent to ruin the lives of the sages: while the sages engrossed themselves in deep meditation to gain higher goals like salvation, Indra was afraid of their austerity which could achieve miracles, for instance, even dislodge Indra from his throne. Hence, the employment of the beautiful nymphs to seduce the high-souled sages of the mortal world. Often the sages succumbed to the sex appeal of the *apsaras*es. Sometimes, the result was just the opposite: the sages hurled curses which brought a lot of suffering upon the *apsaras*es. They were sometimes deprived of their powers (*mahimā*) and had to leave the celestial world and stay in the mortal world in any form — animate or inanimate. Such instances are met with in the pages of the epics and the Purāṇas. Even Urvaśī was no exception. However, her birth or origin strikes a distinct note. She is said to have been born from the thigh of Nārāyaṇa, a great sage. So was born Tilottamā, who was fashioned in a peculiar way by Brahmā himself. But all followed the same lot.

The legend of Purūravas and Urvaśī is first met with in the *R̥V*, 10, 95, which gives us a dialogue in 19 stanzas. It begins abruptly and ends likewise, leaving us to seek help from outside to reconstruct the whole theme. The *ŚB* provides the background of the dialogue and a tenable story could be made. The conditions on which the union of the lovers depended were made to break so that the release of Urvaśī could be effected. Thus, the union of the lovers is found to be short-lived in the Vedic works.

Plunging into the Epico-Purāṇic sources one becomes wonderstruck, with the visualisation of varied versions of the legend.

The *Rām* states a legend where Mitra and Varuṇa competed with one another to share the bed with Urvaśī. Urvaśī became the apple of discord between the two. The result was that Urvaśī had to bear a curse to descend to the mortal world to live for some time with Purūravas. The *Mbh* does not speak of the legend in this way. Purūravas and Urvaśī figure in two different manner in the two epics.

But the Purāṇas are prolific in giving us a running commentary upon the Vedic legend. *ViṣP* tries its best to turn the tragic story into a comic one and succeeds in effecting some changes in the story. It makes the king an adherent of Vaiṣṇavism. The *BhāgP* and others follow the Vedic story. It is the *Vāmana Purāṇa*, followed by the *Devī Bhāgavata*, which describes the birth legend of Urvaśī. She is said to have born from the thigh of Nārāyaṇa. It was also an occasion in which Indra sought to disturb the penance of the sage by sending a host of *apsaras*es to him. But the sage could pre-empt Indra's intention. So he rubbed his thigh and produced a beautiful nymph and presented the same to Indra. As she was born from the thigh, she came to be known as Urvaśī.

The legend is given a better treatment at the hands of the great Indian master poet Kālidāsa, who based his masterpiece *Vikramorvaśīyam* on this memorable piece of legend and imposed immortality on the popular theme continuing from the Vedic works to the classical one. The drama rationalises the conditions and the circumstances leading to the imprecation hurled upon Urvaśī. It also unfolds the truth of the continuity of the lunar line through the progeny born of the union of Purūravas and Urvaśī.

The theme has been an attraction for the modern writers too. Rāmdhārī Singh composed a modern *kāvya* on the basis of the theme without much deviating from the original story. So also Dipak Sen, a Bengālī novelist, wrote his *Urvaśī Jananī*, effecting much innovation in the old story and giving Urvaśī the status of 'motherhood' — which every woman wishes for deep in her heart. Lastly we come across a novel in Assamese by Narayan Kataki entitled *Abhiśata Urvaśī*, with some innovation in the old theme.

The general characteristics of nymphs is reflected in the life of Urvaśī who also, without taking rebirth, changes the body. She is found to bear the character of a hetaera. The behaviour of the *apsaras*es leads one to think whether the *devadāsī*s or temple girls of the later age were a legacy of the tradition of the *apsara*s or not. This induced us to add a chapter on the *devadāsī*s. The popular belief and anecdotes lead one to surmise that the *devadāsī* cult was a remnant of the tradition of *apsaras*es. One can draw parallelism between the *apsaras*es and *devadāsī*s in this way:

(1) *Apsaras* were born to remain unmarried and live the life of a concubine. They could enjoy the company of gods and mortals alike.

(2) They were subjected to strife, and lived an accursed life.

(3) They were devoted to dance and music.

(4) *Devdāsī*s were also born to live in the temples as servants of the gods.

(5) They also remained unmarried throughout life and were enjoyed by priests and other persons.

(6) They are also found to be associated with dance and music.

Thus, Urvaśī and other *apsaras*es made significant contribution to dance and music of the Indian culture. One cannot imagine Indian culture without dance and music. But the life of a dancing girl, whether she was an *apsarā* or a *devadāsī*, appears to have been miserable. Just as a lotus born in mud emits fragrance and charms all people, so also an *apsarā* or a *devadāsī*, born in wretched circumstances, has made a significant contribution to our culture in the form of dance, music and drama.

Appendix I

Genealogy of the Lunar Race

PURŪRAVAS was born as a son of Budha and Ilā and that is why he was called Purūravas Aila. Budha was the son of Candra or Candramas. Purūravas was a prince of the royal family that descended from Soma or Candra. This family was called Candravaṁśa or Lunar race, against the other called the Solar race or Sūryavaṁśa which descended from Vivasvat (Sūrya). However, the Candravaṁśa spread more throughout India in comparison to the Solar race. During the *Mahābhārata* age it swept across almost the whole of India, barring a few pockets in Ayodhyā, Mithilā and Kośala. With the passage of time the Lunar race assumed much prominance. Its princes established new kingdoms all over India and ruled over these.

It is known that Purūravas had begotten several sons in Urvaśī. They were known as Āyus, Dhīmān, Amāvasu, Viśvāyu, Śatāyu and Gatāyu. Āyus, the eldest of all, assumed the kingship after Purūravas' retirement to the forest. In fact, he consecrated his son before his retirement. Many a great king was born in this line, and each of them left a glorious history behind to be remembered by the posterity. They were the great integrators in those times. It, however, is not possible to draw a long historical picture in this dissertation, and it is not the proper place to draw such a picture. The genealogical table is drawn below to show as to how the family grew to a great extent and held sway over the country.

Candra (Tārā)

Budha (Ilā)

Purūravas (W.Urvaśī)

Āyus Amāvasu Dhīma Viśvāyu Śatāyu Gatāyu

According to the Brahma Purāṇa — Solar race

Kāśyapa+Dākṣāyaṇī

Vivasvan

Manu Vaivasvat Śradhādeva Yama Yamunā

Ilā + Budha

Purūravas + Urvaśī

According to the Viṣṇu Purāṇa — Solar race

Brahmā

Dakṣa Prajāpati

Aditi

Sūrya

Manu

Ilā + Budha

Purūravas + Urvaśī

According to the Harivaṁśa — Solar race

Kaśyapa + Aditi

Visvasvan

Manu Vaivasvat Śrādhadeva Yama Yamunā

Ekṣāku Nābhāja Dhṛsun Śaryāti Nariṣvau Prāṁśu

Nabhajariṣta Karuṣa

Praśadhra Iḍā Ilā + Budha Purūravas + Urvaśī

According to the the Agni Purāṇa — Solar race

Manu-Vaivasvat

Ekṣāku Nābhāga Dhṛṣṭa Śayyāti Prāṁśu Ilā Budha

Purūravas + Urvaśī

Śiva Purāṇa - Solar race

Kāśyapa

Vivasvan

Vaivasvat + Manu

Ekṣāku Śibi Nābhāga Dhrsun Śayyāti Narasyata Nābhāga

Karuṣa Priyavat Ilā or Iḍā + Budha

Purūravas + Urvaśī

Mahābhārata — Solar race

Praceta

Dakṣa

Aditi + Kāśyapa

Sūrya Iḍā or Ilā + Budha

Purūravas + Urvaśī

Mahābhārata - Candra (Moon) Dynasty

Soma (Moon)

Iḍā or Ilā + Budha

Āyu Dhīman Amāvasu Dṛhāyu Vanāyu Śatāyu

Harivamśa - Moon Dynasty

Prajāpati

Atri

Soma (Moon) + Tārā

Budha + Ilā

Purūravas + Urvaśī

Āyu Amāvasu Viśvāyu Śrutāyā Dṛhāyu Vanāyu Śatāyu

The Viṣṇu Purāṇa Moon Dynasty

Nārāyaṇa

Brahma

Atri

Candra (Moon) + Tārā

Budhat Iḍā or Ilā

Purūravas + Urvaśī

Āyu Dhīman Amāvasu Viśvāyu Śatāyu Śrutāyu

Śrīmadbhāgavata Purāṇa - Moon Dynasty

Parama Puruṣa

Sayaṁbhū

Brahmā

Atri

Soma (Moon)

Budha + Ilā

Purūravas + Urvaśī

Agni Purāṇa : Moon Dynasty

Viṣṇu

Brahmā

Soma (Moon)

Budha + Ilā

Purūravas + Urvaśī

Āyu Dṛhāyu Aśvāyu Dhanāyu Dutimān Vasu Dibijāta Śatāyu

Genealogy of Purūravas

According to the Viṣṇu Purāṇa

Chandramas family (Lunar dynasty)

Brahmā

Atri + Anusūyā

Soma or Candra

Candra + Tārā

Budha + Ilā

Purūravas + Urvaśī

Āyus Dhīmat Amāvasu Viśvavasu Śatāyu Śrutāyu

Amāvasu

Bhīma

Kāñcana

Suhotra

Jahnu

Sunaha

Ajaka

Balakāśva

Kuṣa

Kuśumbha, Kuśanābha, Amūrtāyu, Amāvasu

Kuśāśva

Gādhi Kauśika

(Gādhi + Satyavatī)

Ṛcika

Kṣatravṛdha

Suhotra

Kasahesu, Ghṛtsamada

Kāśa

Dhīrghatamas

Dhanvantarī

Ketumat

Bhīmaratha

Divodāsa

Pratardana

Alarka

Santali

Sunītha

Suketu

Vibhu

Subhibhu

Sukumāra

Dhṛṣṭaketu

Vanahatia

Bhaga

Bhargabhani

Purūravas + Urvaśī

Agni

Nahuṣa, Keśara, Vividha

Rambhā, Ragi and Annas

Sons of Āyus

Nahuṣa

Yayāti

Yāti

Sañjyāti

Āyali

Viyāti

Kṛti

Yayāti + Devjānī, Śarmiṣṭhā

Nadu, Turvasu

Yayāti + Śarmiṣṭhā

Dṛvhāyu, Anu, Puru

Puru, son of Yayāti and Śarmiṣṭhā

Janmejaya

Praśinvat

Pravīra

Marsasya

Bhayada

Sudarmana

Bhāhagāva

Sanyāti

Ahanyāti

Raudraśva

Reteyaḥ, Kākṣeya, Sthāndileyu, Ghṛtāyu, Jāleyu, Sthāleyu and others.

Rantinara

Tanśu, Apratiratha, Dhruva

Aprativatha

Kāṇva

Tansu

Anila

Duṣyanta + Śakuntalā

Bharata

Bharata sacrificed to the Marutas, obtained by

Bharadvāja, Vitatha

Bhavanamanyu

Vr̥hatkeṣatra, Mahāvīryya, Nara and Garga

Nara

Sanskr̥ti Garg Mahāvīryyu

Ruchivadhi, Rantideva Sini Urukṣāyu

Kroṣṭr̥

Vr̥ñjinisat

Svāhi

Ranshadra

Citraratha

Śaśavindu

Pr̥thuyaśas Protherkarman, Pr̥thajaya Pr̥ther Kr̥tti

Pr̥thadana Pr̥thasuavas

Urukṣya

Jaryyuraṇa, Puṣkarain, Kapi, Vr̥htakṣatra

Sahotra

Hastin

Ajamīḍha Dvividha

Purumīḍha

Ajamīḍha

Śāradvata or Gautama + Ahalyā

Śatānanda

Satyudhṛti + Urvaśī

Kṛpa and Kṛpī (were born)

(And from) Ajamīḍha

Ṛkṣa

Saṁvaraṇa + Tapati

Kurin

Sudhonsh, Jahnu, Parīkṣit

Suhotra

Cyavana

Kṛtaka

Uparicara

Pratyagru, Kusumba Ma Vella, Matsy and others

Vṛhadratha

Kuśāgra

Ṛṣabha

Puṣpavat

Satyadhṛta

Sudunavān

Jantu

Vṛhadratha had another son named Jarāsandha, who become famous for his unique valour and power, and fought against Kṛṣṇa and Balarāma and was killed by Bhīma in a duel fight, which is described in the Sabhā Parva of the *Mbh*.

Jarāsandha

Sahadeva and others

Kuru

Parīkṣita

Janmejaya, Śrutasena, Ugrasena, Bhīmasena

Jahnu

Suratha

Vidūratha

Vidathin

Bharadvāja

Vitatha

Bhūmanyu

Bṛhatkṣatra

Suhotra II

Hastina

Ajamīḍha	Dvimīḍha (Dvijamīḍha)	Purumīḍha	Samīḍha
Nīla	Manva	Ṛkṣa	
Śānti	Medhātithi	Sanvaraṇa	
Suśānti		Kura	
Purujanu			
	Sadhanu	Jahnu	
Tṛkṣa	Suhotra III	Suratha	
Bhṛmyasva		Cyavana	Vidūratha
		Kṛmi	

Mudgala Sṛñjaya Yayiyana Bṛhadisa Kāmpila Sārvabhauma

Vadhryasva

Divadāsa(s) Ahalyā(D) Jayatsena

Mitrāyu	Rucira
Maitreyu	Bhauma
Sama	Tvaritaym
Sṛñjaya	Akradhana
Cyavana	Devatithi
Sudāsa	Dakṣa
Suhadeva	Bīmasena
Somaka	Dilīpa
Janta	Pratīpa
Pṛsata	Śāntanu
Drupada	Vicitravīrya
Dhṛṣṭadyumna	
Dhṛstaketu	Dhṛtarāṣṭra Pāṇḍu

Duryodhana (99 brothers)

Yudhiṣṭḥira Bhīma Arjuna Nakula Sahadeva

Abhimanyu Suhotra IV

Adapted from Dr. T. Sarmah, *The Bharadvājas in Ancient India.*

Appendix II

An alphabetical list of apsarases

Adṛākā
Agastyā
Alambuṣā
Ambhagā Nandanā
Ambikā
Amalocā
Anavadyā
Añjanā
Anucānā
Anukā
Anūpā
Anuvācā
Anuvāsā
Anuvṛtā
Ariṣṭā
Arjunī
Aruṇā
Aruṇapriyā
Arupā
Asitā
Cārunetrā
Caruñjā
Citralekhā
Citrāṅgadā
Citrasenā
Daṇḍagaurī
Dantā
Devisālā Stakatā
Divyā
Gandhakālī
Gaurī
Ghṛtācī
Ghṛtasthalā
Gopālī
Granthinī
Guṇakeśī
Guṇamukhyā
Guṇavarā
Hastinī
Hṛddedakṣarā
Iralonapādi
Kāmyā
Karandhamā
Kavikā

Keśinī
Kṣemādivī
Kumbhayoni
Lakṣaṇā
Latā
Manoramā
Manu
Maricī
Menakā
Miśrakeśī
Mṛgapriyā
Nandā
Parṇinī
Prajāgarā
Pramāthinā
Puṇḍarikā
Puñjikasthalā
Pūrvacittī
Rambhā
Ṛtusthalā
Sahajanyā
Sannāpi
Śāpasenā
Śāradvatī
Saurabheyī
Somā
Śrīṇiḥ
Subāhu
Subhadrā
Subṛtā
Sugandhā
Sugrīvā
Sugurni
Sulikā
Sulocanā
Supriyā
Surasā
Surathā
Svāhā
Svayamprabhā
Umaloca
Urvaśī
Urvī
Vāmā
Vaṁśā
Vapaṣṭamā
Vapu
Varginī
Varuthinī
Vāsī
Vidardhā
Vidyutā
Vidyutparṇā
Viśvācī
Vudavudvalatā

Bibliography

A. Original texts and commentaries

Agni Purāṇa, ed. Baladeva Upadhya, Varanasi, 1966.

Atharvaveda, Paippallāda Saṁhitā, ed. Raghuvira, Lahore, 1963-42, vols. I-VIII.

Atharvaveda, Śaunaka Saṁhitā, with Sāyaṇa's Commentary, ed. Visva Bandhu, Hoshiarpore, 1960-4.

Bhāgavata Purāṇa, Nirnaya Sagar Press, Bombay, 1950.

Bṛhaddevatā, ed. and tr. (Eng.), A.A. Macdonell, *HOS*, vols. V-VI, Reprint, Delhi, 1965.

Brahmāṇḍa Purāṇa, ed. J.L. Shastri, Varanasi, 1973.

Brahma Purāṇa, ed. (tr. Hindi) Tarahisv Jha, Prayag, 1976.

Daśakumāracarita of Daṇḍin (Sanskrit Sahitya Sambhara), vol. VII, ed. G.N. Shastri, Calcutta, 1986.

Harivaṁśa Purāṇa, BORI, Poona, 1969.

Jaiminīya Brāhmaṇa, ed. Raghuvira and Lokesh Chandra, Nagpur, 1954.

Kādambarī, ed. Pandit K.M. Sastri, The Chowkhamba Sanskrit Series Office, Varanasi 1, 1961.

Kādambarī, M.R. Kale, Motilal Banarsidass, Delhi, Patna, Varanasi, 1968.

Kauṭilya Arthaśāstra, ed. R.P. Kangle, Bombay University, Bombay, 1960.

Kauṭilya Arthaśāstra, (Ass. tr.) R.K. Devasarma and Dr. D. Sarma, Publication Board, Guwahati, Assam, 1978.

Kāṭhaka Saṁhitā, ed. S.D. Satavalekar, Auudh, 1943.

Kathā-sarit-sāgara, 3rd. edn., K.N. Sharma, Sarasvata, Patna, 1974.

Mahābhārata, vols 1-18, ed. Sukthankar, BORI, Pune, 1944-66.

Maitrāyaṇī Saṁhitā, ed. Satavalekar, Ananda, 1942.

Mārkaṇḍeya Purāṇa, ed. Pancanana Tarkaratna, Calcutta, 1983.

Nirukta and Nighaṇṭu, ed. and tr. (Eng.) L. Sarup, Reprint, New Delhi, 1967.

Raghuvaṁśa with Mallinatha's *Sañjivanīṭīkā*.

Rāmāyaṇa, ed. H. Bhatta, and others, vols. 1-7, Oriental Institute, Vardodara.

Rāmāyaṇa, Makhanlal Sen (tr. Eng.), Rupa & Co., Calcutta, Allahabad, Bombay, New Delhi, 1989.

Ṛgveda Saṁhitā with *Vedārtha Prakāśa of Sāyaṇa*, 4 vols, ed. Max Muller, Varanasi, 1960-3.

Ṛgveda Saṁhitā, with *Vedārtha Prakāśa* of *Sāyaṇa*, ed., C.G. Kashikar and Santakke, vol. 15, VSM, 1933, !931.

Ṛgveda Saṁhitā with the commentaries of Skanda Svāmin, Venkata Madhava, Mudgula and Udgitha, ed. Vishvabandhu, Hoshiarpur, 1760-63.

Ṛgveda Sarvāṇukramaṇikā, Madhava Bhatta (ed.) C. K. Raja, Madras, 1932

Sāmeveda Saṁhitā, S.D. Satavalekar, Pardi, 1957.

Śatapatha Brāhmaṇa, ed. Rajendralal Mitra, New Print, Delhi, 1972.

Śatapatha Brāhmaṇa, ed. Weber, Chowkhamba, Varanasi, 1964.

Sāhitya Darpaṇam, ed. B.K. Mukhopadhyaya, Calcutta, 1979.

Skanda Purāṇa, Gurumandala Series, Calcutta, 1960.

Śukla Yajurveda, *Sarvāṇukramaṇī Sūtra*, ed. S. D. Satavalekar, Auudh, 1925.

Taittiriya Brāhmaṇa, Anandasrama Press, 1934.

Tāṇḍya Mahābrāhmaṇa, Chowkhamba, Varanasi, 1935.

Vājasaneyī Saṁhitā, ed. S.D. Satavalekar, Pardi, 1957.

Vaṁśabrāhmaṇa with *Devatadhya Saṁhitopanisad*, ed. B.R. Sharma, Tirupati, 1965.

Vikramorvaśīyam of Kālidāsa, ed. M.D. Paradkar and others, Bombay, 1971.

Vāyu Purāṇa (1) Mansukh Roy, Calcutta, 1957; (2) Anadāśrama Press, Poona, 1908.

Viṣṇu Purāṇa (1) Purana Prakashana Mandal, 1903; (2) Sri Ram Sarma, Bareilly; (3) Sanskriti Santhan.

B. Books

Agrawal, V.S., (1) *Matsya Purāṇa*, A Study, Varanasi, 1963; (2) *Vāmana Purāṇa*, A Study, Varanasi, 1964; (3) *India as known to Panini*, Varanasi, 2nd edn., 1963

Awasthi, A.B.L., *History from the Purāṇas*, Lucknow, 4th August, 1975.

Banerjee, P., *Apsarās in Indian Dance*, New Delhi, 1982.

Banerji, A.C., *Studies in the Brāhmaṇas*, Delhi, 1963.

Chakravarty, S., ed., *Saura Purāṇa*.

Dange, S.A., *Pastoral Symbolism from the Ṛgveda*, Univ. of Poona, 1980.

Dange, S.A., *Vedic Concept of Field and the Divine Fruitification*, University of

Bombay, 1971.

Dange, S.A., *Legends in the Mahābhārata*, Motilal Banarsidass.

Dandekar, R.N. (1) *Vedic Bibliography*, vol. I. Karnataka Publishing House, Bombay, 1946, vol. II, Reprint, vol. 4, BORI, Poona 44, 1985; (2) *Vedic Mythology*, Trans. Ajanta Publications, Delhi, 1979.

Das, A.C. (1) *Ṛgvedic Culture*, R. Cambray 69, Cal. 1925; (2) *Ṛgvedic India*, Motilal Banarsidass, Varanasi, 1971.

Dinakar, Rāmdhārī, *Urvaśī* (Hindi Kāvya), Patna, 1986.

Dey, S.K., *Ancient Indian Erotics and Erotic Literature*, K.L. Mukhyopadhyaya, Calcutta.

Deshmukh, P.S., *Religion of the Vedic Literature*, London, 1973.

Devasthali, C.W., *Religion* and *Mythology of the Brāhmaṇas*, University of Poona, 1965.

Diksitar, V.R.R., *Matsya Purāṇa, A Study*, Madras, 1935.

Diwekar, H.R., *Ṛgveda Sūkta Vikāsa* (Hindi), Delhi, Motilal Banarsidass, Delhi, 1970.

Drurry, Niama, *The Vedic Ṛṣis*, Queensland, Australia, 1975.

Dutta, R.C., *History of Civilisation in Ancient India*, London, 1931.

Eggeling, J., tr., *Śatapatha Brāhmaṇa*, SBE vol. XIL, Varanasi.

Ghosal, U.W., *Studies in Indian History and Culture*, Calcutta, 1965.

Griffth, R.T.H., *The Hymns of the Ṛgveda*, Motilal Banarsidass, Delhi, 1969.

Grigwold, H.D., *The Religion of the Ṛgveda*, Motilal Banarsidass, Delhi, 1969.

Hopkins, E.W., *Epic Mythology*, Chowkhamba S.S., Varanasi, 1974.

Handique, K.K., *Naiṣadhacarita of Śrīharṣa* (tr. Eng.) Deccan College Post-Graduate and Research Institute, Poona, 1965.

Kantawala, S.G., *A Cultural History from the Matsya Purāṇa*, M.S. University, Baroda, 1964.

Kapadia, B.H., *Viśvāmitra*, Sardar Patel University, Vallabh Nagar, Gujarat, 1971.

Karambelkar, V.W., *History in the Atharvaveda*, Nāgpur, 1974.

Keith, A.B, (1), *The Religion and Philosophy of the Vedas and Upaniṣads*, HOS, vols., Motilal Banarsidass, Delhi, 1970; (2) *Ṛgveda Brāhmaṇas*, Motilal Banarsidass, Delhi, 1970; (3) *Veda of Black Yajus School* (Eng. tr.), Delhi, 1967.

Keith and Macdonell (in collaboration) *Vedic Index of Names and Subjects* (2 vols., reprint), Delhi, 1967.

Kosambi, D.D., *An Introduction to the Study of Indian History*, Bombay, 1956.

Law, N.N., *Age of the Ṛgveda*, Firma K.L. Mukhopadhyaya, Calcutta, 1965.

Macdonell, A.A., (1) *History of Sanskrit Literature*, Motilal Banarsidass, Delhi, 1965; (2) *Vedic Mythology*, Indological Book House, Delhi, 1963; (3) *Vedic Reader*, Oxford, London, 1970.

Majumdar, R.C. and Pusalkar, A.D., ed., *The Vedic Age*, Bharatiya Vidyā Bhavan, Bombay, Fourth Impression, 1965.

Mani, Vettam, *Purāṇic Encyclopaedia*, Motilal Banarsidass, Delhi, 1975.

Max Muller, F.A., *History of Ancient Indian Literature*, Revised by S.N. Shastri, Chowkhamba S.S., Varanasi, 1968.

Monier, Williams, M.A., *Sanskrit-English Dictionary*, Motilal Banarsidass, Delhi, 1963.

Oldenberg, *Ancient India — Its Language and Religions*, Calcutta, 1962.

Pargiter, F.E., *Ancient Indian Historical Tradition* (reprint), Delhi, 1962.

Patil, D.R., *The Cultural History from the Vāyu Purāṇa*, DCRT, Poona, 1947.

Pillai, G.K., *Vedic History, Set in Choronology*, Kitabsthan, Allahabad, 1959.

Pusalkar, A.D., *Studies in Epics and Purāṇas of India*, Bombay, 1955.

Sarmah, T., (1) *The Bharadvājas in Ancient India*, Delhi, 1991; (2) *Veda Kānanar Ekañjalī Phul*, Sarbhog, 1987 (in Assamese); (3) *Vaidik Kāhinī Pravāha*, Guwahati, 1991 (in Assamese).

Siddhantalankar, S., *Heritage of Vedic Culture*, Bombay, 1969.

Smith, Vincent, *A Early History of India*, 4th edn., Oxford, 1924.

Sorensen, S., *An Index to the Names in the Mahābhārata*, reprint, 1963.

Tilak, B.G., *Vedic Chronology and Vedāṅga Jyotiṣa*, Poona, 1965.

Tripathy, K.S., *A Cultural Study of the Śrīmad Bhāgavata*, B.H.U. Sanskrit Series, vol. IV, Varanasi, 1969.

Trivedi, D.S., *Indian Chronology*, Bombay, 1963.

Upadhyaya Baladeva, (1) *Ācārya Sāyaṇa aur Mādhava* (Hindi), Prayag, 1949; (2) *Purāṇa Vimarśa*, Varanasi, 1965.

Vaidya, C.V., *History of Sanskrit Literature*, Vedic Period, Poona, 1930.

Whiteney, W.D., *Atharvaveda Saṁhitā* (tr. 2 vols) reprint, Delhi, 1962.

Wilson and Others, *Matsya Purāṇa* (tr.) Oriental Publishers, Delhi, 1972.

Wilson, H.H., (1) *Viṣṇu Purāṇa* (tr.); (2) *Ṛgveda* (tr., vols. 1-6) Poona, 1925-28, reprint, Delhi, 1972.

Winternitz, N., *A History of Indian Literature*, tr. into English by Mrs. S. Ketkar, University of Calcutta, 1927.

C. Articles

Alsdure, L. Hanburg, The Ākhyāṇa Theory, *Reconstructed Journal of the Oriental Institute M.S. University*, vol., XIII, No. 3, March 1964.

Bhat G.K., A thought of Saṁvāda Sūkta, *Journal of the University of Bombay*, vol. XXVIII, Part 2, Sept. 1959.

Banerjee, S.C.K., Music and Dance in Ancient and Medieval India, *Akhil Bhāratīya Sanskrit Pariṣad*, Lucknow, December, 1979.

Bordoloi, Pavan, Udice Nṛtyar āt Bicāri, *Raṅghar* 13th Yr, No. 8, January 1994, Guwahati.

Bordoloi, Pavan, Devadāsī Jivan Kathā, *Raṅghar*, 13th Yr., No. 7, December, 1993.

Borodoloi, Pavan, Manipurar Devadāsī Prathā, *Raṅghar*, 14th Yr., No. 3, June 1994.

Baruah, Madhav, *Devadāsī Nṛtya Paurabicitrā*, 22nd Year, No. 8, Guwahati, 1983.

Baruah, Tultul, Devadāsī Nṛtyar Ādi Pārvan, *Dainik Janambhumi*, Jorhat, 29th Yr., No. 166, 18 Nov., 1990.

Chattopadhyaya, A., *The Institute of Devadāsī*, M.S. University Baroda, Baroda, 1946.

Chaliha, Pradip, Asamar Mandirar Nṛtyar Śeṣa Star-Devadāsī Nṛtya, *Adhināyaka*, Ist Yr., No. 10, No. 1989.

Chaudhuri, Medini, Prācin Bhāratya Samājat Nācar Ṣtḥān, *Jātiya Sāhitya Pariṣad*, Guwahati Sahitya Sabha, 1st Publication, June 1989.

Chaudhury Aruna, Prācin Bhāratīya Nṛtya Kathār eti camu Paricaya, *Asam Lekhak Samabai Samity*, 1st Publication, June, 1989.

Chutia Makat Siṅgha, Āntarjātic Nārī āru āmi, *Natun Dainik*, Guwahati, 8th March, 1991.

Chapekar, N.G., Apsarā, *Poona Oriental*, vol. XXIII, No. 1-2, January-April, 1988.

Dange, S.A., Urvaśī, the Water Belle, *Journal of Oriental Institute*, vol. XXV No. 1, Baroda University, Sept. 1975.

Deva Chandra Paresh, *Devadāsī Nṛtya Chanda Śilpa*, 1st Yr. No. 4, July 1991, Jorhat, Assam.

Devi Rajani, Hindu Dance (*Apsara Dance*), Sunit Publication, Delhi, 1920.

Datta, Sudhindranath, 'Urvaśī' Poem, *Sudhindranath Dattar Kāvya Saṃgraha*, Deys Publication, 1st Publication, 1369, May, 1962, Calcutta.

Daya, Sabitri, Ādhunik Hindi Mahākāvyame Nārī Devarajar Prakasan Yoypur 6, 1977.

Daloi, Sarmah Harinath, Vikramavaśīr Kāvyik Samdarya — article, *Rāmdhenu*, 14th Yr. No. 3, 1983.

Dixit, V.V., *Relation of Epic Brāhmin Literature*, vol. VII, April, July, 1942.

Gaur R.C., The Legends of Purūravas and Urvaśī, *RIHS*, Session, 1968.

Goswami, Susil, Āmbarir Purātvātik Khanankārya, *Prakash*, 13th Yr., No. 9, July, Guwahati, 1988.

Handique, K.K., Women Poets of the Ṛgveda.

Hariyappa H.L., Ṛgvedic Legends through Ages, *BOCRI*, Poona, 1951.

Kaṇbalkar, V.W., Purūravas And Urvaśī, *All India Oriental Congress Conference*, 1961.

Kalita Tikendranath, Devadāsī Nṛtya, *Dainik Janambhūmi*, Oct., 6, 1991.

Kakaty, Dilip Kumar, Devadāsī Nṛtya, *Dubi Devīlaya Bajali Darpan*, 53th Session, Pathsala, 1987.

Karmākar, D., Urvaśī Purūravas, *Journal of Bombay Branch of Asiatic Society*, No. 271, 1951.

Kosambi, D.D., An Introduction to the Study of Indian History, Bombay, 1956.

Louis Renou, Vedic India, Indological Book House, Delhi, 1971.

Nalini Indira, Legends of Purūravas and Urvaśī, *JUB*, 19 Sept., 1950.

Patra Jivan Krishna, Bajalir Nṛtya Kathā, *Pāthśalā Sānskritik Samāj*, Pāthśālā, Kāmrup, 1982.

Pillai, K.K., The Temple as a Cultural Centre, Part — vol. LVX, No.3, Madras 1960, Bombay Journal.

Patawari, Rupsri, Devadāsī Nṛtyakathā Prāgjyotishiyā, Session 24th, Guwahati, 1988-90.

Sastri, Rangapal, Purūravas aur Urvaśī Kā Akhyāna, *Hindi Vedavani*, 24th January, 1972.

Sastri, Haraprasad, Urvaśī Vidayā Haraprasad Racanavali 1363, Bangavada, Eastern Trading Co., Edited by S.K. Chatterjee, Anil Kr. Kanojilal.

Shastri, P.S., The Ṛgvedic Ballads, *The Poona Orientialist*, vol. X, 3-4 July-Oct., 1945.

Shastri, P.S., The Ṛgvedic Lyrics, vol. XI, No.2 October, 1945, *Quarterly Journal of the Mystic Society*, 1949.

Shastri, P.S., The Dramatic Fragment of Ṛgveda, *Bhāratiya Vidyā*, vol. XVI, No.2, Bombay, 1956.

Shastri, P.S., The Ṛgvedic Poetic Spirit, vol. XXVIII, Parts I-II, Poona, *Annals of Bhandarkar Oriental Research Institute*, 1957.

Shastri, P.S., The Saṁvāda Sūkta of the Ṛgveda, All India Oriental Conference, 13th Session, Nagpur University, 1946.

Sripath, Devadāsī, Historical Article, *Ānandabājār Patrikā*, Śāradiya, Calcutta, 1372.

Sarmah, T., Purūravas aru Urvaśī (Āssamese) Prakāsh Publication Board, Guwahati, Ṛgveda + Saṁvād Sūkta.

Tagore Rabindranath, 'Urvaśī', Poem Sancyyita, *Viśvabhāratī*, Calcutta, 1961.

Tripathy, V., Urvaśī tathā Vāk, Hindi p. 24, Alok 25, 1968.

Vimala, Vaidik Sāhitya me Urvaśī aur Purūravas.

Wright, A.C., Purūravas and Urvaśī, *BSO*, AS. 3. 526. 547, London University, 1967.

D. Articles

1. Aurobindo, 'Urvaśī', Poem, vol. 5, Aurobindo Āśram, Pondicherry, India, p. 119, 1972.
2. Baruah, D.K., Devadāsī Poem, Sāgar Dekshisā, Lowyer's Book Stall, Guwahati, 1945.
3. Baruah, Ananda Ch., 'Urvaśīlai', Bakulbanar Kabitā, Assam Prakasan Parishad, Guwahati, 1976.
4. Borodoli, Nirmal Prabha, 'Urvaśī. One Act Play', Nilachal.
5. Datta Sudhindranath, 'Urvaśī Poem', Dey's Publication, 1962, Calcutta.
6. Gogoi L., Devadāsī (Story), *Natun Dainik*, 10th March, 1972.
7. Kalita Ramesh Ch., Devdāsīr Prem (Novel), Assam Book Depot, Guwahati, 1990.
8. Hajarika, Atul Chandra, Devdāsī, Assam Kurisatikar Asamiya Kabita, Assam Prakadan Parisad, Guwahati, 1977.
9. Neog Dimbeswar, Śāpamukta Urvaśī Asana, Jorhat, 1924.
10. Mukhopadhya Nirmal, Abhiśapta Urvaśī, Play, Rajendra Library, Calcutta 132, 2741.
11. Mukhopadhya Apareshandra, Urvaśī Gitinatya, *Sahitya Parisad Patrika*, Calcutta, 1919.
12. Sarma Bani, Nistabdha Nupur (Novel on Devdāsī), Ganthapith, 1984.
13. Sanyal, Avanti, 'Hājar Bacarer Premar Kabitā' — Purūravas Urvaśī, Visvani Prakasan, Calcutta, 1974.
14. Sharma S., Institution of Marriage in the Vedas with Special Reference to Women's Status, *Sadhaak*, A Journal of Historical Research, vol. 21, Part C, Sl. No. 63, 1992, Gandhi Nagar, Jaipur, India.
15. Tagore, Rabindranath, 'Urvaśī' Poem, Sancayita, Visvabharati, Calcutta.

Index